WHAT
MEN
WANT

WHAT MEN WANT

Bradley Gerstman, Christopher Pizzo
and Richard M. Seldes

PIATKUS

Copyright © 1998 by Bradley Gerstman, Esq.,
Christopher Pizzo, CPA and Rich Seldes, M.D.

First published in Great Britain in 1998 by
Judy Piatkus (Publishers) Ltd
5 Windmill Street
London W1P 1HF

First published in the United States
in 1998 by Cliff Street Books, an imprint of
HarperCollins Publishing, Inc.

The moral right of the authors has been asserted

*A catalogue record for this book is available
from the British Library*

ISBN 0-7499-1915-9

Jacket design by Ken Leeder

Printed and bound in Great Britain by
Mackays of Chatham PLC, Chatham, Kent

In memory of Connie Clausen

CONTENTS

ACKNOWLEDGMENTS

I would like to thank my mom and dad, for everything; my sister Linda, my brother Danny, and his wife, Pam, for their advice and love; and my law partner, Michael, for his support. And special thanks to Cheryl, for walking into my life at the perfect time.

—Bradley Gerstman

Thank you to the most important woman of all, my mother, Barbara, for always being there. To my dad, thank you for your confidence in me and continuous motivation. You truly are my best friend. And by the way, pass on a word of thanks to Ruby Bagonia. Thanks also to my grandparents, Sue and Sal, whose fifty-six years of marriage are an inspiration to us all.

—Christopher Pizzo

Thanks to my mom, dad, and grandmother for their love and support. And special thanks to Marla, my best friend and love of my life, for her sweetness and enduring patience.

—Rich Seldes

All three of us would like to give special thanks to Rosalind Arden whose expert editorial guidance and sensitive "woman's ear" did much to improve the content and cadence of our prose. We thank Stedman Mays and Mary Tahan at Connie

Clausen & Associates Literary Agency for their hard work, good humor, and for carrying on and keeping Connie's spirit alive. We thank our editor, Diane Reverand, and the staff at HarperCollins for their expertise and for believing in us. And, finally, thanks to all the women in our past and present, you know who you are.

WHAT MEN WANT

One

INSIDE THE MIND AND HEART
OF THE PROFESSIONAL MAN

Have you ever wondered why a man cheats on the woman he loves? Or why, after having passionate sex, he bolts out the door like a track star? Why a man doesn't enjoy talking about "the Relationship"? And why he has so much trouble saying "I love you"? Have you ever considered whether you should offer to pay for something on a date? Or whether having sex too soon could sink a relationship? Why wouldn't a guy call after what appeared to be a great first date? And is "playing hard to get" really worth the effort?

When women ask these questions, men's lips are usually sealed. When it comes to revealing their emotions toward women—whether vulnerability, ambivalence, or delight—men usually adhere to a code of silence and appear indifferent. Men are *not* indifferent. Beneath that silent, tough exterior, he is a human being as fragile and vulnerable as you are. In *What Men Want*, we break the male code of silence and reveal what's behind that macho facade.

We are three single, professional men—Brad's a lawyer, Chris is an accountant, and Rich is a doctor—and our book provides the road map to the hearts and minds of professional men. Our advice is not written by someone outside the dating scene looking in. Nor is it a list of old-fashioned, outdated rules recorded by women who claim to know what men want. We are men speaking directly to a woman, having that conversation her boyfriend usually avoids. We open up and speak honestly—without pulling punches—about how men think and feel, how we act and react.

Some readers will be shocked. We don't camouflage the fragility of men's egos. We don't soften the rawness of men's sex drive. Knowing the reality—*not the ideal*—of what men want can free women to make better decisions in their love relationships. Knowing the truth about men can help women stop being hurt by the men who don't love them, and can help them keep the men who do.

As three bachelors who have been in love—and are experienced in the dating scene—we're struck by how often the opposite sexes get their signals crossed. Men and women just can't read each other right. The magnitude of the problem hit us one summer when we shared a beach house with a diverse group of single women. While sitting around the pool, walking on the beach, or having a few drinks before hitting the town, conversation inevitably turned to relationships. Our women friends confided in us their troubles with the men they were dating, and we found ourselves explaining how men think and feel.

Our friends asked us to be frank with them—and we were. We told them the ugly truth when it seemed clear they were being blown off, manipulated, or used in their relationships. We also helped them see when their men might be holding back out of insecurity and fear rather than lack of love or desire. We discussed everything from giving out their phone numbers to casual dating, from sex to commitment. Our women friends told us that our summer of talk helped them gain a fresh perspective on why men act as they do. Their newfound understanding of men helped them to improve their good relationships and discard their bad ones.

What surprised us was that they found our information so startling and new, so eye-opening. To us, it just seemed like common sense. We know how guys' brains work. We know what men's hopes and expectations are. But our female friends were shocked and amazed—even doubtful—at first. Our knowledge of what works with men didn't always fit with what *they* thought would work. And what we advised didn't always match what their girlfriends and mothers recommended.

Then they realized that we were *exactly* the kinds of guys they were dating. They were in relationships with stockbrokers and engineers, lawyers and doctors—professional men just like us. They knew they could trust and rely on our reading of their boyfriends' points of view. So our women friends started putting our advice to work. And you know what? Immediately, their love lives started to improve.

Knowing what men want helped them maximize the happiness and minimize the pain of their love relationships. And at the end of that summer, during a "farewell to summer" Labor Day dinner, our women friends suggested we write a book. "Get the information out," they told us. "Women need it."

All our advice follows one simple principle: *Weed out Mr. Wrong, nurture Mr. Right.* Let us explain. We have found— from our own dating experience, and from what our women friends tell us—that too many women get stuck in relationships going nowhere. If this happens to you, just follow our advice about how to weed out Mr. Wrong and you'll save yourself some time and protect yourself from unnecessary pain. Many women also—without meaning to—ruin a good thing and end up alienating the men who do love them. If you worry that you might be driving away the man you love, read carefully what we say about nurturing Mr. Right.

Who is Mr. Wrong, anyway? He's the guy who strings you along with no intention of getting serious. He's the guy who's wasting your precious time. Our friend Valerie needed help in weeding out Mr. Wrong. She had been dating a guy for two months. They were sleeping together, and she was falling in love with him but she worried that he didn't feel as serious about her as she felt about him. She asked us what we thought.

We asked her a few key questions to determine whether he considered her a "good for now" girl or a woman with "wife potential." You see, when a man starts dating a woman, he immediately determines which category she fits in—and treats her accordingly. And a man's behavior is a dead give-away to whether he is serious about a woman or just stringing her along.

Did she see him on weekends or just weekdays? Were their conversations always short and not too profound or did they have conversations about serious things? Did they ever talk about the future? Had she met his parents? Did he phone in advance for dates or did he often call after midnight wanting to come over right away and have sex? Her answers made it clear where she stood with him. We advised her that if she was looking for marriage—and not just some fun—to drop him, because she was one of many women on his dating list. He was treating her like a "good for now" girl. And she would never be anything more to him.

The situation was different with Anna. She needed to nurture her relationship with Mr. Right. She and her boyfriend had been dating for a year and were clearly in love. But she was frustrated because she wanted to "speed things up and get married already!" That was how she put it. How could she get him to pop the question? What in the world could she do?

Well, after talking for a while it became clear to us that her boyfriend had actually been gearing up for the final count-down to asking her to marry him. Like many women, she was freaking out because he was taking so long to get to the point. Unfortunately, her pressure was forcing him to clam up! Her need to know and her desire to talk about the rela-tionship all the time had even driven him to stop saying "I love you."

We told Anna to relax, stop hounding him, and let love take its course naturally. Things could be speeded along, but not by pressuring him. If she wanted that engagement ring, the best thing for her to do was *be* all the things he loved her for in the first place. If he liked her cooking, then she should cook for him. If he liked her easygoing, cheerful self, then she should be happy and cheerful with him. If he loved her in sexy lingerie, she should go out and buy some more. That was in May. By August, her new, relaxed attitude had allowed *him* to relax. Once the pressure was off, he was able to bring up their rela-tionship in his own way. He started saying "I love you" again. He started sending those bouquets of flowers she loved. The last we heard, they were in Venice on their honeymoon.

Frankly, when you know what a man wants, it's easier to get your own way with him. A man needs to feel he's mak-ing his own decisions in his own time. That is why trying to force a man to do something will always fail—even if he wants to do it! A man also needs to feel liked and needed. That is why "playing hard to get" is a bad idea.

Our friend Deborah complained to us about the trouble

she was having developing and maintaining relationships with men. When we pressed her for details, we discovered that she was treating men like adversaries. She often played hard to get in an effort to keep a man interested. Early in the relationship, she made sure to curb her enthusiasm. Later on, if the guy was still around, she used jealousy as a ploy to inflame his passion.

Deborah was pulling back in an effort to draw men in closer. But her efforts to spur men to the chase only succeeded in chasing them away. When men stopped pursuing her after a few dates, she wondered why. It was clear to us that Deborah was alienating men by striking at the heart of their insecurity. Contrary to what her girlfriends may have counseled, or self-help books may have proclaimed: *Playing hard to get doesn't work.*

As a rule, men do not reveal their vulnerability, so women fail to see it. We understand that women need to protect themselves from men who might take advantage of them. We know that women too often get involved in relationships with men who are not serious about them. But why alienate a man who has the potential for being the man of your dreams? By playing hard to get, women often do themselves, and men, a disservice. There needs to be more generosity between the sexes, not less.

What motivates a guy is a woman's genuine kindness. When you do nice things for a man, all of a sudden it becomes easy for him to do things for you. This is just common sense. All guys know that in the long run, when a woman plays hard to get, it doesn't work. Our fathers, our coaches, and our friends have told us what it's like to be in a good relationship. They've clued us in to how we'll know when it's really right versus when it's just okay. "The girl you marry should fit you like an Armani suit," they say.

Unfortunately, dating a woman in the nineties sometimes feels like wearing a suit from the seventies. It just doesn't fit right.

This book doesn't seek to pit the sexes against each other. We think there has been enough of that. Instead, we seek to throw up the white flag, to surrender the battle plan: We show women what men *really* want. Instead of scaring off interesting guys, women can learn to read the signals men send. If you do that, *you can master the art of weeding out Mr. Wrong and nurturing Mr. Right.*

Susie was completely baffled when a guy she had three great dates with stopped calling her. There are a few reasons why a man will stop calling, but we knew Susie pretty well. "Did you talk a lot about your ex-boyfriend?" we asked. She had. When Susie liked a guy, she dug right in and discussed deep, personal topics on the first few dates. Like many women, she believed talking about her ex-boyfriend was a good way to share her feelings and bond with this new man. We advised Susie to stop talking about the ex. And sure enough, although she never heard from that guy again, she followed our advice with a new man she met. They are now dating seriously.

Men are easy to read once you know their language. We've listed clear signals men send when they love women and when they don't. Women who can read these signals will be better able to disentangle themselves from relationships destined to fail. By helping women read men better, our book will also enable women to start and sustain relationships with the men who love them. We tell women the things they do to drive us away. And we tell them what it is they do that captures our hearts.

We are not psychologists. Our expertise lies in our status as "regular guys" who love and are loved by women. We are the guy in the suit on the subway, the clean-cut guy drinking Dewar's at the bar, the athletic guy jogging in the park. We are also the guy in the restaurant treating his mother to Sunday brunch, or out hitting golf balls with Dad. We are ambitious, well-educated, family-oriented men. Our book sheds light on what all men want, but we won't presume to speak for all men. We speak for men like ourselves, typical professional men who are cut from the same cloth.

What kind of woman is the professional man looking for? In general, the professional man likes a woman who is easygoing and fun loving. He prefers a woman who is open-minded, not prejudiced. He is thankful when a woman is stable, intelligent, and has a good sense of humor. He seeks a woman he can be proud of in the company of his boss. He is attracted to a woman who is sexy, health conscious, and secure within herself. And he loves a woman who is generous, caring, and sincerely interested in him.

But don't misunderstand us: Professional men are not perfect, and they are not looking for a woman who is perfect. In fact, you're going to see some of our foibles up close and personal. Here's who we are:

Brad: We think of Brad as the "player" or—as he matured—the "reformed player" among us. He is a sharp dresser, the headstrong type, and he loves to debate. In college, he played football, won a student athlete award, made the dean's list. After practicing law as an assistant district attorney in the Bro   nd started his own law firm, Raskin & Gerstman,   P n the past few years he has played the field and has had a few serious relationships. Despite his tough exterior, Brad is sensitive to the needs and wants of those he loves.

Chris: We think of Chris as the "romantic" among us who, against all odds, has achieved a lot. After being raised by a single mother on a limited budget, Chris was determined to succeed. After college, he passed the CPA exam, completed his MBA, went on to work at a big-six accounting firm, and is now a vice president of finance. In college, he played football and then fell in love in his senior year. When that relationship ended four years later, he put a Band-Aid on his heart and started looking for Ms. Right. He has been actively dating ever since. Chris's open-heartedness sometimes leaves him feeling too vulnerable to the hurts inflicted by others, but his affectionate nature and direct style win him the friendship of many who know him.

Rich: We think of Rich as the "intellectual" among us. He is cultured, well traveled, and appreciates the finer things in life. As president of his college fraternity, member of his college football team, and summa cum laude graduate, Rich has always led by example. Rich went on to medical school to become a doctor so that he could affect people's lives in a positive way. In medical school and as a physician, Rich needed—and had trouble finding—a woman who gave him the space and time to pursue his career. After years of dating women who played games, he finally met Marla, his girlfriend for the past three years. As a surgeon and as a man, Rich proceeds with a measured pace and a steady hand.

Now that we have introduced ourselves, we will tell you what men want. Most men don't tell women much of what they are thinking and feeling. Perhaps we don't think about, and certainly don't say out loud, the male code by which we live—we just live by it, *religiously*. In any case, it's time we let women in on a few facts.

Two

TEN FACTS ABOUT MEN

FACT NUMBER 1

Women Have More Power Over Men
Than They Know

Did you know that it is easier for a man to take a swing at a guy twice his size, ask his boss for a raise, and run a marathon on a hot day than it is for him to approach a woman? Men are trained and biologically driven to be aggressive and competitive. But in his mind you are more daunting than a six-foot-six football tackle or a roomful of demanding business associates. He can sustain bodily injury, he can negotiate business demands, but he can't risk his manhood where it's most vulnerable. With you.

Of course, a man's sense of himself as a man is also gained by competing with other men, by doing well in the world, and by his own sense of dignity and worth. But his manhood is most vulnerable when he measures himself in the eyes of women, or of one woman. No matter how confident, good-looking, or successful a man is, he will always worry about saying something stupid to a woman and embarrassing himself. Men's powerful desire for women is matched by our equally powerful insecurities.

Women too often think men hold all the power in relationships, but the truth is that women hold enormous power. A woman has the power to invigorate a man or to crush him. Is it any wonder men are so self-protective and careful when it comes to choosing the women they will marry?

A woman who knows the power she possesses over a man can channel that power to win his mind and heart. Tap into that power and you've got the man.

FACT NUMBER 2

Men Appreciate Women Who Take the Initiative

Some women believe that men are threatened by assertive women, but the man who is your equal will appreciate your taking the initiative. Don't just be chosen, choose. Men of character believe in a balance of power.

This is true even during that first encounter between a man and a woman. Men have an internal calibration system that measures whether or not we should approach a charming stranger. If you are interested, go ahead and tip the scale in your favor. You have the power, so use it. Once you understand how insecure men really are when it comes to women, it makes sense to use your power and signal your interest. Since men are such acute readers of women's body language, a look will often be enough to get him moving across the room in your direction. Men love women who show an interest in them. Isn't it human nature?

Men Are Turned Off by Women Who Play Hard to Get

Men are suspicious of women who play hard to get. Flirting is fun; don't get us wrong. But being charmingly reserved is one thing and being downright manipulative is another. If a woman thinks a relationship would have worked out had she played harder to get, she is wrong. Relationships are formed and sustained by chemistry and hard work. To be sure, it's human nature to want what you can't have, and so posing a challenge might indeed make a man chase. But if there is no chemistry, no substance once the chase is over and the challenge conquered, the relationship is destined for failure anyway.

Many professional men don't have time for games and won't stand for them, and they may jump ship when they see games being played. A woman playing hard to get may not even be giving herself a fair chance to make it work with a great guy. Men don't want to risk being shot down by pursuing someone who appears unattainable. Just trying to meet and have a relationship with a woman is a challenge in itself. There is no need to play hard to get. Wouldn't a woman want to know sooner rather than later if the relationship was going to work out? Playing hard to get is a waste of time and prevents a man and a woman from getting to know each other.

Of course we're not suggesting you throw caution to the winds when you meet a new man: Just be real. A man will like you more if you are caring and sincere. Machiavellian manipulation tactics will get you nowhere.

FACT NUMBER 4
Men Will Take Advantage of Women Who Let Them

We are sorry to say that many, if not most, men will take advantage of those women who will let them. Women waste a lot of time in dead-end relationships when it is as plain as day that the guys are stringing them along. A man who is happy with the relationship as it is can linger forever maintaining the status quo. You must draw the line, because he won't. But we are pleased to say that men respect and respond to your boldness and self-respect. Give wake-up calls to men you believe may be playing games with you. If you suspect you are on a man's "good to have around until something better comes along" list, confront him. Men have less of a problem than women do in staying in "fun for now" relationships. He is perfectly content but needs to know if you are not. When asked point-blank what his intentions are, a man will be on his honor to tell the truth.

But he might soften his language to shield you from the blow. And in the pages that follow we'll clue you in on what statements like "I am not ready for commitment" really mean. We will also help you identify the physical, verbal, and emotional clues that tell you he thinks the relationship is on its last legs.

FACT NUMBER 5

When It Comes to Sex, Men Still Believe in the Double Standard

Men don't tell women what they really think about the do's and don'ts of sexual behavior because we don't want to incite a riot. Political correctness has not yet entered the bedroom. A man still holds a woman to a stricter sexual standard than he holds himself to. This means that the timing of the first sexual encounter will influence the way he feels about you. If you have sex with him too soon, he will be less likely to consider you as a potential girlfriend or wife.

The truth is that while men talk fast and seductively, deep down they are conservative and idealistic about the kind of woman they will marry. Men talk one game, but keep a sharp eye on what a woman does. If they've known you a week and know your body intimately, they may not care to cultivate your mind. Practicing caution at the beginning of a relationship allows a woman to weed out the guys who are ambivalent, the ones who want only sex, the guys who are not right for her.

But if you too are a sexual predator, men will be game. Just know what to expect. The chances are that he won't want a long-term relationship with you.

FACT NUMBER 6

Men Are Extremely Jealous, So Trying to Inflame His Jealousy Will Always Backfire

Professional men are competitive and hate to lose—or even think of losing—what they have. If he is jealous, he is struggling with the thought that he thinks there is someone out there who can make his girlfriend happier and treat her better than he can. This is mental torture at its most subtle and strikes at the heart of a man's fear: He is not man enough to make the woman he loves happy.

That's why it's a mistake to try to use jealousy as a ploy to reel him in closer. A man will drop a woman cold rather than suffer this kind of torture. One of us had a girlfriend once who constantly tried to make him jealous. Her behavior made him resentful and insecure; it also made him think *she* was insecure. He reacted by trying to meet and date other women. Nobody enjoys being made to feel jealous. The ultimate question is: How could making a sane man jealous possibly make him love a woman more? If a woman feels there are problems with her relationship, she should confront her boyfriend with those issues rather than playing the jealousy game.

Men who are too possessive are men who are insecure. And there are a lot of those men out there. Calm his fears by telling and showing him how much you care. If he is too possessive and *continually* limits your freedom, drop him.

FACT NUMBER 7

Men's Natural Inclination Is to Have Sex with Many Women

Many men keep their relationships monogamous by satisfying their need for variety through pornography and by going to strip clubs. Looking at different naked women satisfies a man's visual imagination. And, of course, all men masturbate.

But a man unchecked is a man who will spread his seed. A man will be polygamous unless something or someone restrains his natural inclination. That could be religious values, or a vow of loyalty. Many men will cheat anyway, scoundrels that we are. What inhibits many is fear: fear of losing the woman we love. Not only that, but fear of the emotional pain that losing the woman we love will make us feel is also an inhibiting factor. Some men run after pleasure wherever they can find it. If they were sure that their wives or girlfriends would never uncover their infidelities, many men would have sex with other women. That's the ugly truth.

FACT NUMBER 8

Men Have a Hard Time Interpreting Women's Talk

Watch his facial expressions as you discuss problems in your relationship. Pain, puzzlement, and, finally, *relief* when you get to the point and state what it is you want him to *do*. For women, the value of talk lies in the process of talking. But men are goal-oriented, so talk feels like a waste of time. Or, worse, a man perceives your request for more talk as a demand or a complaint.

Know that when you talk as you naturally do, a man often finds it difficult to understand you. He senses all sorts of things circulating beneath the surface of your conversation, but he is not sure what or even where they are. When you say, "Let's talk about our relationship," he thinks, "What's wrong, what does she want me to say, to do? How does she want me to change?"

Men are trained at practical problem solving, so we respond best to clear-cut requests. In chapter 7, we give advice on how to bring up the delicate topic of commitment so that your man will be able to hear you, understand your feelings, and be considerate of them.

The key to better communication with a man is to be direct and loving.

FACT NUMBER 9

Men Would Rather Be Intimate
Than Talk About It

Don't believe that men fear intimacy. Men are cautious about displaying vulnerability, but we are not cowards. And, after all, men need women. What is true is that men are poor emotional communicators. It is difficult for men to actually say "I love you" no matter how powerful our feelings for you. We sympathize with women and understand that it is important for them to hear declarations of love. As often as we are able, men do try to say "I love you" to make women happy. Unfortunately, we are not able to do this very often. A woman should know a man loves her by what he does and by the look on his face every time she enters the room. Most men will show their love in deeds, not words.

The Way to a Man's Heart Is Through His Ego

Any man will be drawn to a woman who thinks and cares about him. Men marry women who are loyal and supportive. They need their wives to be *on their sides*. A man will not hook up with a woman who constantly tears him down—he simply can't afford to. His ego couldn't sustain the lifetime siege. We're not saying that men and women shouldn't negotiate, argue, scream, and yell once in a while. But, basically, a man seeks a harmonious relationship. He needs harmony at home so that he can go out into the world with his best self intact. A man knows when a woman isn't really on his side but is only *saying* she is to get whatever it is she wants from him, whether it be sex, money, or an engagement ring.

When we say the way to a man's heart is through his ego, we don't mean that you should waste your breath flattering him all day. We don't mean that you should efface yourself in order to build him up. What we mean to say is that a man will love a woman whom he feels he can make happy. Think about the look on his face when he brings you flowers. He is *pleased*. Not only is he happy to make the woman he loves satisfied, he is pleased to know *he can please you*. So let him know when he does.

• • •

These are some basic facts about men. In the pages that follow, we will map the anatomy of a love relationship, from the first encounter to the marriage proposal, showing at every level of intimacy what men want and think, how they act and react. Once you see the *reality* of what men want, you can work with the facts. Once you know the facts of a man's desires and fears, he's yours.

Three

THE FIRST ENCOUNTER

Men feel the spark of sexual attraction either immediately or never. This is what fuels the chemistry of a memorable first encounter. When he sees that special someone across a crowded room, he will *feel* the impact. His knees may buckle slightly. His heart will beat faster. As his body temperature increases, he will start to sweat. This is not just excitement, it is nervousness. When men feel that spark of attraction, we become excited *and nervous.* We are fine talking to a woman we are not interested in. It is the woman we *really* want to meet who makes us tongue-tied. Right away, we put her on a pedestal. We erect a barrier of fear and desire that may become difficult to break through. As soon as the spark is lit, our confidence tends to plummet, we lose our rap, and we become fearful, fumbling idiots. Sometimes we lack the courage to go up and meet her, sometimes we manage to propel our bodies across the room and introduce ourselves.

Once we start talking with her and the conversation flows, after 60 or 120 seconds, the barrier is broken. We sigh with relief and think, She is human. If we are lucky and all goes well for another half hour, we happily think to ourselves, She sees in me what I see in her—we're getting along. This is chemistry. What sparks it is sexual attraction. What sustains it is compatibility.

Even when the spark is there, men approach far fewer women than we would like to. Remember those times when you sensed that a guy wanted to meet you, but he just never stepped up and introduced himself? He stared at you. He may even have angled his way to your side of the room. Then . . . nothing. Perhaps you thought you were imagining things: The eye contact was accidental, he was staring at the basketball game on the screen above your head or at the blonde next to you. Don't fool yourself. He was dying to meet you. He just couldn't muster up the courage.

The man knows he is supposed to approach the woman, not the other way around. Men are taught from day one to be aggressive. We are supposed to be strong, confident, able to control our own destinies. Yet meeting women is not as easy as it looks or sounds. We feel frustrated when we think of all the women we've wanted to approach and yet never managed to meet. These are women glimpsed at business conventions, in department stores, at the gym, in bars, in subways, at the laundromat—anywhere. The point is that when you compare how many women men *actually do* approach to the many women men *want to* approach, the number is astonishingly low. We would venture to guess one in twenty, maybe even one in forty. This may surprise you. As a woman, you may be thinking, What are men so afraid of? Do they think women bite?

How a Man Decides to Approach a Woman: The Imaginary Balancing Scale

Let us tell you how men think. That charming stranger you wish to meet has in his mind's eye a precisely calibrated scale by which he measures whether or not to cross a crowded room and introduce himself. Picture it—as the weight piles on one side, the scale tips that way: She'll reject me. I'll make a fool of myself. Is that a wedding ring on her finger? As weight is placed on the other side, the scale begins to come back into balance: There's nobody sitting next to her. She's definitely looking at me. Maybe it's just a school ring.

When we contemplate meeting a woman, we pile all of the positives on one side and all of the negatives on the other. If the scale favors approaching her, we will. If the scale favors minding our own business and leaving her alone, we won't approach her. Should I or shouldn't I? Sounds simple, right? Well, it's a lot more complex than it sounds.

What Keeps Men Away: The Negative Weights

First of all, the scale does not start out balanced. Fear of rejection weighs so heavily that, from the outset, the scale leans in favor of not risking an introduction. We can't tell you how many times we've thought, Better not risk it. A man *hates* to be rejected by a woman. And, by nature, men are insecure. It is amazing how insecurity can turn a school ring into a wedding ring from only two feet away. No matter how rich or famous or good-looking or brilliant, a man will always wonder: Does she have a boyfriend? Will she blow me off? Does she hate men? Is she in a bad mood? The most common reason men give for not approaching women we want to meet is fear of rejection.

Men also feel the need to impress a woman, so we put a lot of pressure on ourselves. We want to say something that sets us apart from the other hundred guys who are trying to achieve the same goal. If we convince ourselves that we won't say something stupid, then we are afraid that whatever we do say will not be well received.

Remember the scene from *About Last Night* when Rob Lowe and Demi Moore were staring at each other from across the bar? After a cat and mouse game of staring at each other and looking away, Rob got up the courage to go talk to Demi. He had a brilliant opening line, something like, "I couldn't help notice you noticing me." Demi responded by telling him she wasn't staring at him, she was staring at the clock over his head. Not only did he have a stupid line, it wasn't well received. This is every man's worst nightmare.

Unsuccessful attempts at trying to meet women can have a devastating effect on a man. He will lose confidence. He will kick himself. Worse still, rejection has a cumulative effect: I'm such a loser. Each time he is rejected, it stays in his mind and makes it that much more difficult to approach another woman the next time: Never again. I'd rather go home and masturbate. The weight on the negative side of the scale gets heavier and heavier and harder to offset with positive things. He now needs a bulldozer to take the bricks off the negative side of the scale. Being rejected never leaves his mind. Whether up front in his conscious thoughts or buried in his subconscious fears, rejection is always there.

Certain situations tip the scale in favor of minding his own business and leaving her alone. Time is usually not on a man's side when it comes to meeting a woman. Is she on an elevator, in a subway? He thinks, No way. Not enough time to give my best rap. He will probably not risk starting a conversation only to have it end seconds later when the elevator reaches her floor or the subway pulls into her stop. Location too is often inhibiting. Women have a legitimate fear of strangers, especially in big cities, and men respect that: She'll think I'm an ax murderer.

Men also don't like to approach women if there are a lot of people around. It is difficult to talk to a woman for the first time at the gym or at the beach, or in any other crowded area. If he is at a gym, it seems to him that everyone has stopped working out and is hanging on every word he says. If he is at the beach, it seems to him that the pounding ocean waves have stilled themselves to allow everyone to listen in and judge his every word: Everyone is staring at me, waiting for me to get shot down. A man's self-consciousness in a crowd can make an already awkward situation more uncomfortable.

Piling on the Negatives: Girls' Night Out

A solid brick is placed on the negative side of his imaginary scale when a man sees a woman he would like to meet hanging out with the girls. Whether it is a "bachelorette party," a birthday party, or a reunion of college friends, girls' night out is an incredibly intimidating scenario for most men. We are not saying that you shouldn't go out with the girls. We certainly understand the value of friendship. We are saying that if you are out with the girls, and do see a man you would like to meet, it is probably best if you step out of the group.

While we were discussing writing this book, the three of us went out to dinner one night to a good family-style

Italian restaurant on the Upper East Side of Manhattan. Wouldn't you know it, we were seated right next to six beautiful women who were there for a birthday celebration. They were drinking wine, telling stories, and laughing. It appeared that the last thing on their minds was meeting guys. No man in his right mind would have approached any woman in this crowd.

We thought about it, though. We thought about sending a bottle of wine over to their table. We thought about a lot of things. When the waiter came over and asked what we'd like, all we wanted to say was "Them." All we managed to say was "Um." We were so distracted we couldn't even order our food. In the end, we were too intimidated to act. We were too overwhelmed by our terror of the spotlight and our fear of rejection. All we could do was stare at these beauties and watch quietly as they paid their bill and left.

Chris recently went against the norm and actually tried to meet a woman on girls' night out. Of course it was a mistake. He was at a dance club on a night when the club was throwing a party for the Elite Modeling Agency. There were beautiful women all around the bar, dance floor, and lounge area. Chris managed to make eye contact with a woman he was interested in meeting. She was dancing with five other women. He watched as she turned away three other men who dared approach. But he was determined to test this theory one more time. And she was stunning. Against all odds and with all of the weight on the negative side of the scale, Chris stepped up to meet this beauty. The inevitable happened. She was polite but unreceptive. She was at her girlfriend's birthday party and just did not want to be bothered by men.

It's difficult to meet a woman when she is out with the girls. Knowing this, most men will not even try. We feel it is a no-win situation. So, if you do see a professional man you are interested in meeting while you are out with the girls, you need to take action. You need to knock that brick off the negative side of a man's imaginary scale by making it easy for him to approach you.

How to Meet a Guy When You Are Out with the Girls

The way to meet a guy when you are out with the girls is to step aside, get away from the pack for a while. Don't appear glued to the other women you are with. Instead, go to the bar to get a drink or stand near the dance floor by yourself. Just opening up space for a man to approach you is usually enough for a man who has already spotted you and wants to meet you. If it is not, you can glance in his direction, stand near him, or even start a conversation with him.

Use the security and energy of being out with a group of your friends to your advantage. Step out of the group with one of your girlfriends. Both of you can then make eye contact with the guy you want to meet. Your friend can introduce you, and then, eventually, get out of the way.

If he is with a male friend, you and a girlfriend can glance in their direction or stand nearby. Your friend can begin talking to his friend, paving the way for you to meet him.

Using friends to help you meet guys can change what was an impossible situation for meeting men into an optimum one. Guys use their friends to help them break the ice with women all the time. Women can, and should, do it too. It works!

The Protective Friend:
The Policewoman Who Keeps Men at Bay

Even more frustrating than trying to meet a woman in a group is trying to meet a woman and having to battle her protective friend. Don't get us wrong, going out on the town with a close friend is a great way to meet new people. We are often drawn to two attractive and vibrant women out together. But the protective friend (aka Ms. Policewoman) is something else entirely. You all know about the protective friend. Perhaps you have played this role yourself on a few occasions. Rather than invite men into the fold, Ms. Policewoman poses a major obstacle to any man trying to get to know her friend.

A man knows he cannot battle a protective friend. His job is to win her over so that she doesn't drag you away from him. He will try to keep your friend engaged in the conversation so that she doesn't feel neglected or left out. If your friend isn't won over, and you are not helping him out conversationally, a man will quickly bail out of this situation. A man will give up rather than battle an unhappy friend. Having an overly protective friend around when you are trying to meet the professional man of your dreams is like trying to run a marathon wearing five-pound ankle weights.

While on a business trip in Nashville, Tennessee, Chris went to a local nightclub with a few coworkers after an all-day meeting. He spotted a nice-looking woman he wanted to approach. He knew he was flying out the next morning and that nothing serious was likely to result from the evening. Since he was writing this book, he thought it would be a good time to prove the "protective friend" notion to himself outside his usual stomping grounds. Sure enough, nothing was different.

He approached the woman and began talking to her. She was extremely friendly, and had a nice southern accent and a cute smile. The conversation went well until, out of nowhere, the woman's friend came over and dragged her away without even saying "Excuse me." As it turned out, she dragged her into the bathroom to gossip about nothing. When the woman returned, she apologized to Chris for her friend's rude behavior. Our theory was confirmed even outside our usual territory.

Brad engaged in a similar battle recently in a lounge located in downtown Manhattan. He approached a woman he thought had been smiling at him during the course of the night. He introduced himself and she invited him to sit down. Almost immediately, Brad could feel the tension emanating from the woman's friend. Brad went out of his way to include her in the conversation, but all he got was curt, snobby answers. Her attitude did not make it easy for Brad to get to know the one he was interested in.

As the night progressed, Brad asked the woman to dance, thinking this would provide him with an opportunity to get this young lady away from her hostile friend. As she got up to go with him to dance, her friend followed. The three of them made their way out onto the crowded dance floor, and before the song ended, the woman's friend was complaining that the place was too crowded and that she was tired and wanted to go home. Brad was in a no-win situation. What was he to do? He made every attempt to get the woman he liked alone so he could get to know her better, but Ms. Policewoman would not allow it. Shortly after their stint on the dance floor, the two women wound up in a fight with each other and left.

That woman allowed her friend to ruin an opportunity for her to meet a man she appeared interested in. If she had allowed herself to step away from her friend, or had flat out told her friend to give her ten minutes to herself, she and Brad might have had a fighting chance of getting to know each other a little better, or at least have exchanged phone numbers or planned to meet another night. We understand the importance of being loyal to your friends. But we advise women to protect themselves from overly protective friends.

There are a few brave men who will—without any positive encouragement—approach a woman out with her friends. But the rest of us need some sort of signal. Women need to give men some encouragement when the potential for rejection is high. So, give him some encouragement. When you are out with a group of friends, you need to step away from the group for a while and give him a chance to approach. Otherwise, that handsome man with soulful eyes and the hopeful look will be unlikely to approach you. If your girlfriend is acting hostile because a guy is paying attention to you and not to her, make it clear that you're interested in talking to him. *If you are out with your friends and see a man you would like to meet, you must let him know it.*

How to Meet a Man Even When You Are Out with an Overly Protective Friend

First, try to avoid the situation altogether by having an agreement with your girlfriend about whether you are going out just to be with each other or are open to meeting men.

If a man appears interested, but your girlfriend is acting hostile, keep the conversation flowing and reward him with smiles, glances, or a touch on his sleeve or hand.

If your girlfriend absolutely does not want to be left alone, and a guy wants to be alone with you, briefly take him aside and tell him what's happening. You might say that you can't leave your girlfriend but that you'd like to see him again.

If you have a tendency to cling to your girlfriend, remember that when she leaves you to dance with a guy, this is a great opportunity for a guy to approach you. Sip your drink demurely and wait.

Don't be nervous. The man who has been eyeing you all night has been waiting for this moment.

Being Categorized Too Easily: The Live Wire

Although men do need encouragement from women during that first encounter, some women go overboard and come on to men in a sexual manner. A man may love an opportunity for an "easy score," but we don't recommend this approach if you are trying to land a professional man for a long-lasting relationship. First impressions are lasting. We are not saying you should be prissy, but going overboard will not send the appropriate signals to a professional man, even if it makes you the life of the party.

Of course, drunkenness never conveys a good impression. And like it or not, most people think a drunk woman is less socially acceptable than a drunk man. Some women (men too are guilty of this) seem to believe that drinking to excess conveys their capacity for being fun loving, unrestrained, ready to live in the now. But nobody likes a drunk. A man wants a respectable partner, not an embarrassment. If you act like a live wire, sure, you may have men all around you paying you a lot of attention, but believe us, this is not the kind of attention you want.

We know of many examples, both firsthand and from many of our friends, that can attest to the live wire situation.

Most, if not all, of these relationships never made it out of the bedroom. We know a guy who was dating a girl who appeared very promiscuous right from the start. He had met her at a Christmas party. It was at a small bar, and she was very drunk. He was very drunk as well, and they kind of hit it off, as best you can under those circumstances. They had a very strong sexual attraction that was consummated that very night.

As time went on, she grew attached to him, while his feelings for her went the opposite way. Although he liked this woman for a short period of time, he could not get past the fact that she had that live-wire streak. She always enjoyed getting very drunk and going to bars to shoot pool and play darts. There is nothing wrong with shooting pool or playing darts, but we think that for him she was more of an embarrassment, while she thought she was being a fun girlfriend. That relationship did not last very long, and she wound up getting hurt when he told her he didn't want to see her anymore.

Professional men do want girlfriends who know how to have fun, but we like women who know and understand where to draw the line. There is nothing more embarrassing for a professional man than to have a wild and crazy girlfriend on his arm, and to never know what stunt she is going to pull next. If you want to meet the professional man of your dreams—and keep him—it's not a good idea to play it like a live wire.

How to Avoid Being Labeled a "Live Wire"

Don't drink to excess. Especially don't chug beer or drink shot after shot of hard liquor.

Don't get involved in dirty dancing, such as grinding against your partner or dancing on the bar or on a table.

Don't fondle or perform sexual acts with a man you've just met.

Don't get involved in sexual conversation, not even sophisticated sexual innuendo.

Piling on the Positives:
How to Tip the Scale in Your Favor

Of course, the live-wire woman is the exception, not the rule, among women. Most women err on the side of passivity, not on the side of aggression. Most women are shy, or appear shy. And with all our talk about men's fear of rejection, you may be thinking it is a wonder men ever approach women at all. Obviously, there is no need for despair. A man's desire for a woman is so strong that it can propel him in her direction against all odds. And women can help. Why risk not being that one in twenty if you spot somebody you might want to talk to? Women can and should beat the odds and tip the scale in their favor.

There is nothing wrong with a woman making the first move. Some women are more aggressive than others and feel completely comfortable in approaching a man. Other women may think that making a first move is not the appropriate thing to do, or may be too shy to do it. We are aware that women have their own fears about signaling their interest: He'll think I'm unladylike. He'll think I'm desperate.

He won't respect me. We understand the societal taboos women must do battle with.

But the truth is, men appreciate it when women are willing and able to make the first move. It shows that you are confident and secure and out to get what you want. It also proves that you are attuned to men's insecurities. You understand that we may need a small signal to let us know we have a good chance of a positive response if we approach you. The bottom line: Men like confident women, and women—who tip the scale in their favor by initiating contact—meet the men *they* want to meet.

Your first move can be subtle or it can be obvious. Initiate things in a subtle way by using eye contact and other body language to propel him in your direction. If you are in the mood for being more direct, you can break the ice with words.

Use Eye Contact to Your Advantage

A woman's glance is a powerful motivator. Eye contact can be a very effective way to convey your interest.

One woman we know tipped a negatively balanced scale in her favor recently in a trendy bar located in the SoHo area of Manhattan. The music was loud and powerful, the bar was crowded with people who looked like they'd come out of a Madonna video. The cigarette smoke filled the bar like a thick rain cloud hovering in the air. Chris spotted an attractive woman sitting on a couch against the far wall. Immediately, his mental calibrations began: First, the scale tipped against approaching her for fear of rejection. It tipped farther when he noticed she was surrounded by girlfriends and sitting in an area that was hard to get to. She also appeared to be deeply engaged in a conversation. Just as he was prepared to forget about her and have her fall into that familiar category of attractive women he would have loved to talk to but never approached, she spotted him. She glanced at him for a second, took a puff on her cigarette, and smiled at him as nonchalantly as a disc jockey spinning one record into the next. To an outsider, the glance and smile would seem inconsequential, nonexistent. However, between Chris and this mysterious beauty sitting on the couch, it was a real signal.

That was all it took to tip the scale in the completely opposite direction. He was now loaded with confidence and ready to meet the woman he had been staring at for the past ten minutes. He approached her, and they hit it off right away. He didn't think she was unladylike for smiling at him, nor did he think she was too aggressive. He was extremely impressed with her ability to be forthright and signal what she wanted. She was a woman of the nineties, confident and strong. She was not prey to old-fashioned beliefs that have become outdated and obsolete. She knew the power of eye contact.

Use Your Body to Let Him Know Your Mind

Here's body language men respond to:

Look at him.

Smile invitingly.

Stand or sit near him.

Raise your eyebrows and tip your drink as if to toast him.

Wave or mouth hello.

Take your headphones off.

Once the two of you are in conversation, touch his arm, hand, shoulder, or back. Smile. Laugh at his jokes. Instead of scanning the room, looking for someone better to talk to, give him your full attention. Stare into his eyes. Flip your hair back, sip on a straw, and look up at him.

Beyond Body Language:
Breaking the Ice with Words

A smile, a glance, and other body language to show that you are aware he is in the room all do wonders to propel him in your direction. In the same way, you can walk up to a man you like the looks of and say hello. *You don't need any elaborate opening lines.* Men don't care what you say. All you need to do is break the ice. All we really register, anyway, is that a woman is initiating conversation. Any of the following simple openers will do:

Hi!

It's so crowded in here, isn't it?

Great tie.

How do you know (fill in host's or hostess's name)?

This band is so loud, I can't hear myself think.

Who do you know here?

We know what you're thinking: I'm afraid to be so forward. What if a guy gets the wrong idea? Guys do not find women who initiate conversations with men too aggressive. The only way a woman can make the wrong impression is by outright sexual innuendo.

If you go up to a guy and say, "Hey, you have a great ass!" yes, you can be sure he's thinking, I'm getting laid tonight. But if you walk up and say hello or comment on something neutral, such as the photograph on the wall, the place you're in, or the music being played, he'll be sure to respond cordially and respectfully. Believe us, it's such a relief when a woman breaks the ice.

We understand that there are deeply ingrained taboos making it difficult for a woman to approach a man. You have to know that a man will understand and sympathize with all the fear and insecurity you had to overcome just to approach him. We've been through it a hundred times, so we know all about it. If he is a man of any character at all, he will be extremely receptive to you. Even if he is not interested, he will not make you feel stupid or rejected. He should be intelligent enough to realize that he needs to help keep the conversation alive. Just sit back, relax, and be yourself. If there is some chemistry between the two of you, or even if there isn't, no professional man with the qualities you are looking for will make you feel uncomfortable or make you regret you made the first move. If he does, then hell, he isn't the guy for you anyway. So what did you have to lose? Some loser who doesn't know how to treat women. At least you gave it your best shot and now know the outcome. If you'd passed up the opportunity, you'd be beating yourself up the next day because you didn't give yourself the chance to meet this potentially great new guy.

When a Man Approaches You . . .

In the same way, if a man approaches you or makes the first move, sympathize with him. Understand that he overcame the fear of rejection and embarrassment to talk to *you*. There was obviously something that attracted him to you, and just the very fact of his coming over to talk to you is a compliment. Put yourself in his shoes, think of all of the weight on the negative side of the scale he decided to ignore, and consider how difficult it was for him to approach and greet a complete stranger. *Remember, it doesn't matter how confident, successful, or good-looking a guy is, the fear of rejection will prevail.* Nor does it matter how successful he has been with other women in the past—he is still unsure of what *you* will say or do or think.

Women should know how much difficulty men have in deciding on an opening line. We don't want to come off as too cocky or confident, we don't want to use some stupid old clichéd lines, and we certainly don't want to embarrass ourselves. However, we do want to say *something* that will grab your attention. We see the opening line as an ice-breaker. And unless it offends, it is usually meaningless anyway.

A simple line is better than an outrageous compliment: "Hi, I'm Brad. What's your name?" He might try to personalize his opening by referring to something specific he notices about you: "Is that Dostoyevsky you're reading?" He may stand near you and listen in on your conversation so that he can pick up clues. If he hears any specific reference, he might interject a comment: "I like seeing live music too, do you know of any good live shows coming up?"

Keep in mind that he is out on a limb. If you are not interested, try not to be rude. Men usually anticipate rejection anyway, and the slightest hint of noninterest, such as short, unresponsive replies, should be enough for him to get the point. If you are rude, it will hurt his feelings and discourage him from approaching other women in the future. You would not want the man of your dreams to pass you by one day because he had just been rudely rejected by another woman.

Try to be courteous; remember that guys are approaching you not because they want to hurt you but because they are interested in meeting you. Don't turn your back on the guy, don't laugh at him. If he is pressing too hard, say, "Thank you very much, but we're leaving soon." Or you might even say, "Your attention is flattering; I do have a boyfriend, though."

Continuing the Conversation: The Script

That first conversation is usually nothing more than an information-gathering session, and yes, most of the time it sounds like a script. We have all been down this road before: "What do you do for a living?" "Where did you go to school?" "Where were you born?" "Do you like sports?" "Do you go to a gym?" Don't think this is a bad rap. This small talk usually leads to more interesting conversation despite how corny it may seem. We call attention to the importance of the script—the trading of vital statistics that happens between strangers—because it seems to us that women usually grow impatient with this sort of talk. They often cut it off too soon and never give a guy a chance.

One woman friend of ours recounted how she met what seemed to be an interesting guy at a bar where mover-and-shaker types went to decompress after work. They struck up an okay conversation, and at one point he asked her, "Do you jog?" Apparently that one question put a halt to any potential relationship the two of them could have had. "Why?" we asked. "Wasn't he good-looking? Wasn't he successful? Hadn't he shown a strong interest in you?" "Yes," she responded. "But I didn't like him making innuendos about my body." The poor guy was just following the script, trying to prevent the deadly pause. He was just making small talk. If you are interested in a guy, know that he's happy to depart from the script, but you'll have to help him.

Men will often throw a compliment at a woman as a test, to see if she responds. It's a verbal cue, a way to open the door—or shut it. If he compliments her and she responds, she may be interested. "You're so beautiful, I wanted to talk to you." "Thank you, you're so kind to say so." If he compliments her and she doesn't respond, or frowns, or gives a curt answer, a man knows it will be an uphill battle. He may cease and desist. Or he may battle on bravely. Women seem to care less than men do about looks and more about conversation. Women judge guys on their raps. One or two curt answers from a woman and a guy may lose heart. So, tip the scales in your favor by using verbal and physical cues to signal your interest.

You will know just how interested you are, so you can determine just how encouraging you want to be. You can show your interest by responding to him not only with politeness but with animation. Be receptive to his compliments and compliment him in return. Answer his questions with interest and energy. Keep the conversation flowing by asking him a question or two. If you like him, reinforce the physical in a discreet way. Turn toward him. As you make a point, touch his hand, sleeve, arm, or shoulder. Flip your hair back, sip your drink, look over at him. Stare into his eyes.

When Rich first became romantically interested in Marla (the woman he now loves), he could easily tell by Marla's actions that she too was interested, and they bonded instantly. Rich and Marla had met briefly through friends at a college bar several years prior to this particular night. They barely knew each other, but recognized each other at a party. Rich's first words to Marla were, "You look fantastic!" Marla replied by saying, "Thanks, it must be my tan. I just got back from Club Med!" This opened up a whole new topic of conversation. And when Marla offered, "You're looking pretty fantastic yourself," Rich knew that this woman was interested. From that point on, they talked all night. Marla laughed at Rich's jokes and made him feel comfortable with her. When one of Marla's friends came over to them, Marla introduced her friend to Rich and then politely gave her "the look"—which meant, "Can you give us some time alone?" It didn't take long for Rich to find out that Marla didn't have a boyfriend, and would be interested in dating him. It was a perfect encounter that led to a serious, committed relationship.

Getting the Number

If a man has had an interesting conversation with you and wants to see you again, he will begin to gather his nerve to ask for your phone number. Again, it is not easy. No matter how well an initial interaction with a woman went, whether at a happening club or at the local supermarket, men will revert to that imaginary scale in their minds when weighing the decision to ask for a woman's phone number. Even if it was the best conversation and there seemed to be chemistry between them, a man is still afraid to ask for a woman's phone number.

This has happened to us, to our friends, to our fathers and grandfathers many, many times. First, we don't want to appear disrespectful. Second, we are afraid you will say no. These are lost opportunities that could be salvaged if men and women understood each other better. If you are interested, give him discreet hints that you might like to see him again or that you enjoyed meeting him. You could say, "I'm so glad we met. We should go hiking one day." Or, "Let me know if you want to go to that concert, I'd love to see that with you." If he doesn't ask for your number after a hint or two, then he is not interested or he fears rejection too much and probably doesn't have any self-confidence. If he does manage to ask you, and you are not interested, it is better to say no than to give him a fake number. Please don't do that.

Of course, many women will not give out their phone numbers to any man after one meeting, and we understand that. It is quite all right to just say no and, if you want it, to ask for his number. Men understand how women feel about giving out their numbers and we don't get insulted. Know, though, that when a woman won't give a man her phone number, but asks him for his, he is convinced that she probably won't call him. You certainly have the right to take a guy's number and not call him: Men do this to women all the time. If you are planning to call (and are not just being polite), we suggest doing something subtle to convince him that you will call, like establishing a day and a time to make the call. Obviously, the most convincing thing you can do would be to call him as you said you would.

That first encounter between a man and a woman should be a balanced give-and-take. Why not establish the harmony of a relationship early on, as early as the first encounter, by encouraging a man? There is no need to be a live wire. When a man meets a new and exciting stranger of the opposite sex, he's an extremely subtle reader of all the signals she may care to send.

The advice we give here may surprise you—but it works. What turns a guy on is a woman who appears interested in who he is and what he has to say. If you stare into his eyes and touch his hand, he will stick around. If you laugh at his jokes and ask him questions, he will want to see you again. Send encouraging physical and verbal cues to men who appeal to you. That way, you will meet the men *you* want to meet. If he doesn't feel the same way, or if he turns out to be not quite what you hoped, you'll soon know. We know that women are taught to fend off men, but you shouldn't fend off *all* men. When a woman doesn't give a man enough encouragement—even when she is interested—a man loses motivation.

Men are taught to pursue women. And we love to pursue women. But you should know that it is not so easy for us to wipe off the feeling of rejection as if it were lint on a suit. Rejection sticks with a guy. Women have enormous power to wound men. That is why we are so cautious when approaching, calling, and dating a woman we like, and marrying a woman we love. So give us some encouragement. All marriages began with a man and woman having that first encounter. The magic usually starts there.

Four

THE FIRST PHONE CALL

After that first encounter with the potential man of your dreams, you will probably begin to wonder when you will speak to him again, if ever. As you analyze the time you spent together, you begin to experience that delicious, awkward, nervous feeling. Is he the one? You may toy with visions of the future. What will you wear on your first date? If you are feeling really imaginative, you may even stop and consider how your first name sounds with his last name.

Generally speaking, men do not think this way. We lack this kind of imagination. A man will not be thinking ten steps ahead, he will be concentrating on that next step. After meeting a woman and getting her phone number, a man will often think no farther than the first phone call. *Should he call her or shouldn't he?* He will immediately begin to debate with himself. To a woman it may seem clear-cut: If the first conversation went well and the two of you appeared compatible, he should, and will, call. Unfortunately, it's not so clear to him. He's not so convinced he will call. Many times, he won't.

Let us explain how a man decides whether or not to call. As when approaching a woman for the first time, he needs to weigh the positives and the negatives. The good news is that this time the scale begins tipped in favor of calling her. If he took her phone number, then he received some encouragement: The first encounter was successful. But that's it. There is no further chance for her to tip the scale in her favor. The bad news is that now he will dream up every reason not to call and see which way the scale is leaning when he's finished.

If you have ever asked yourself, Why didn't he call?, the answer is that he placed too much weight on the negative side of the scale. What makes a man do this and fail to call a woman he likes? Why wouldn't he call?

He May Not Call Because He Fears Rejection

No matter how well the first encounter went, men still dread making that first phone call. If he calls her, he will be placing his cards on the table and opening himself up to possible rejection. His neck will be on the chopping block. As he considers picking up the phone, negative thoughts race through his mind. Will she remember me? Maybe she will screen her calls and won't pick up the phone when she hears his voice. Does she want to talk to me? Maybe she has reconsidered and decided that she doesn't really want to pursue anything further. Should I leave a message? If he does leave a message on her machine or with her roommate, she may not call him back.

Even if he does get through to her, he worries that the conversation may not go well. So what if they had a terrific conversation during their first encounter? Maybe now she will be in a bad mood. Or she might have gotten back together with her ex-boyfriend. The conversation could be uncomfortable, with long gaps and stupid lines pitched just to break the silence.

And there's another daunting thought: Since she doesn't know him particularly well, he will need to make a good impression. He will need to deliver his best rap and provide meaningful conversation. During their first encounter, he had a script to adhere to; now he's going to have to go freestyle. Professional men are used to talking on the phone in stressful situations, but he may not be up for this particular challenging task. If it is the end of a long workday and he is feeling mentally drained, he may just cop out and not call.

But here's the worst scenario: What if she gave him the wrong phone number? If he calls the number and finds this out, *ouch*. We have experienced all of these situations many times. We have met women and had great conversations with them, exchanged phone numbers, even made tentative plans to get together again. Then we decide to call and all we get is the answering machine, day in and day out. Or we call and the conversation is a dead end. Then there are those ego-busting encounters where we have decided to call a woman only to find out that we got the number to some movie theater or shoe repair shop. How humiliating do you think that is for a guy?

After all of these situations, men are left to wonder, Why doesn't she want to talk to me after we had such a good conversation when we met? The way he sees it, it is sometimes just better to cut his losses. Avoid pain, he thinks to himself; don't call.

Fear of rejection really does stop him from dialing your number. That first phone call is never easy to make. All three of us think long and hard about it each and every time. Brad met a great girl who pulled him through his fear of rejection and tipped the scales in favor of his calling her. At their first meeting, they clearly liked each other, but she kept alluding to how busy she was, which made Brad wonder what her point was. Thinking ahead to the moment when he'd have the phone in his hand and an imaginary scale in his head, Brad asked, "Do you think you will be able to fit me into your busy schedule this week?" She looked at him with surprise, paused, and exclaimed, "Yes, definitely!" When he called her, she recognized his name right away. And he felt encouraged by her bubbly enthusiasm. That was much better than hearing, "Who? Oh. Hi. I'm on the other line with a friend from Arizona . . ."

He May Not Call Because He Thinks You're Not His Type

Of course, there are other reasons for a professional man failing to call a woman when he said he would. A man may not call a woman because he is just not interested enough in her. Just as you may get skittish and reconsider your interest in a man after first meeting him, men do the same thing. We think back to that first encounter and realize that she just may not be worth the effort.

A man sees himself as the initiator and motor in a new relationship, so if he can't gear himself up to full throttle, he may decide to turn the engine off. Maybe he's athletic and loves to run and Rollerblade in the park, and she dropped hints that she hates to exert herself physically. Maybe she now seems to him to have been too conservative or too flamboyant for his taste. Maybe he likes to drink and she doesn't, or maybe she likes to go out a lot during the week, but since he is a professional man with a demanding job, he doesn't have the luxury of staying out late on weeknights. Or perhaps the physical and emotional chemistry between them simply wasn't strong enough to make it worth the effort.

While in medical school, Rich met a woman at the local bookstore in the dating and relationships section. This woman was exceptionally beautiful. In a pathetic attempt to start a conversation, Rich asked her, "What's a beautiful girl like you doing in a section like this?" Despite the bad line, she spoke to him and started telling him about her last few boyfriends. All of her relationships had been the same. They would start out as steamy romances and then fizzle out about a month later. She always had a date and was pursued by many men, but she could not understand why she was never in a long-term relationship.

After about an hour of shared conversation at the espresso bar, Rich understood why she never had that lasting love with a man. She told Rich she usually dated professional men. "You know, these professional guys make a lot of money and will treat you right," she continued. But she then went on to complain that they would never talk to her or listen to what she had to say. Rich understood this woman's problem. After the physical infatuation wore off, there was little mental stimulation for her boyfriends. She may have been drop-dead gorgeous, but she was not the brightest star in the sky. After three cups of mochaccino, she said to Rich, "You know, you are a good listener. What do you do?" Rich responded, "I am studying to be a doctor." "That's great. We should go out sometime. Here's my number, give me a call," she said. Rich took the number but never called.

Basically, anything that is important to a man in a woman he dates needs to be there in order for him to pursue her and call her. If she has mentioned anything in the initial meeting that goes against his grain, it is just easier for him not to call. There is nothing a woman can do about this. It is best for her just to be herself and let the chips fall where they may. There is no benefit in trying to be someone you are not just to get him to call you and begin seeing you. Sooner or later your real personalities will emerge and it will be evident that you weren't compatible in the first place.

He May Not Call Because
He's Too Busy, or She's Too Busy

Being too busy will *not* prevent a man from dialing a number he really wants to dial. He can find a minute if he wants to. If he's really taken with you, he will call. But if he's not so interested, a busy lifestyle can get in the way.

The reality of many first encounters is that he just might not know you well enough to feel infatuated. In that case, being busy is a good excuse. He may have planned to call, but then got swept up in an important project at work. His personal life may be on hold while he prepares for eight-hour surgery, argues a tough case in court, or crunches numbers in an effort to prevent the bankruptcy of a major corporation. Now that a week has passed and he has a few spare minutes to call, he worries that the woman won't remember him or want to talk to him after he waited so long.

Or she may have mentioned her own busy schedule. This

happened with a flight attendant Brad once met. [unreadable]
him she was often out of town. Brad decided that it [unreadable]
be difficult to get together with her or have any meaning[unreadable]
relationship with her if she was on the road all the time. In
that case, Brad decided it wasn't worth the effort to make
the phone call.

He Never Had Any Intention of Calling, He Was Only Out to "Get the Number"

Sometimes a man won't call a woman because he never
intended to call her and was only out to get her phone number. Why would a man do this? Men need to know that we
are desirable to women, and so we may at times go out to
meet a woman just to prove that we can. It sounds disgust-
ing, self-centered, and inconsiderate, but we are sorry to say
it is the truth. We have been guilty of it, and we know of
many friends who are guilty of it as well.

Most guys we know have met women and had very good
conversations with them. As the conversation progressed, it
has made them feel good that a woman appeared interested.
So a guy says to himself, Why stop here?, even though he
knows he is not really interested in her. It's fun to flirt.
Sometimes this is taken to the extreme: A guy will ask a
woman for her phone number or mention getting together
for lunch or for a drink. As soon as they part, he will lose the
number; he never had any intention of calling. Men who are
guilty of this tend to be guys who have girlfriends.

When a man has a girlfriend, especially one with whom he
is serious, he constantly considers the idea of never again
being with another woman. This is a scary thought. In order
to ease the pain of never being with another woman, he will

neet other women. He will prove to
ble to other women and ensure that
here he could date if, God forbid, he
rent girlfriend. Again, it sounds very
sh, but men do it all the time.

have for women who give out their
ask the guy for his number in return. If
he hesita   't give you his number, then he wasn't
planning to call you. He either has a girlfriend or is just out
to stroke his own ego. He never had any intention of pursuing anything with you, he is just relieving his own insecurity
at your expense.

What Encourages a Man to Call

When he is sitting at home with the phone in one hand and
your phone number in the other, painstakingly deciding
whether or not to call, he will weigh every detail. That is
why we recommend letting a man know you like him during
your first meeting.

First, because men are men, he will think back and
remember what attracted him to you and how you
responded to him physically:

She's pretty . . .

She laughed at my story about the jokers at work . . .

She touched my hand . . .

Before she left, she took my hand and stared up at
me . . .

She kissed me on the cheek . . .

When I kissed her on the lips, she responded . . .

The most reinforcing gesture a woman can make, which will almost ensure that a man will call her, is to give him a small kiss on the cheek or even on the lips. Yes, if your first encounter is full of fireworks, you can even kiss him on the lips. First encounters like this are rare, but they do happen. You know the chemistry is happening when both of you feel and express an immediate sense of rightness and fun, when the world gets blurry and it's only the two of you.

Of course, if it's a very short or neutral encounter, there is no need to end it with a passionate kiss. But if you like him and the two of you have spent an hour talking, when the time comes to say good-bye, lean over and give him a kiss on the cheek. When deciding whether or not to call you, and struggling with the fear of rejection, he will remember that you kissed him good-bye. He will know that a woman who was not interested in him would never have given him a kiss good-bye. If you like him, but don't feel ready or willing to kiss him, you can take his hand and hold it for a few seconds as you say good-bye. Don't give him a business handshake, though. To him that means business, or friendship.

As he sits, phone in hand and your number before him, he will also think of what you talked about and how you responded to him verbally:

She seemed interested in that story I was telling her . . .

She asked me about my work . . .

She said she'd love to go running in the park with me . . .

What encourages a man to call is his desire and your positive reinforcement during that first encounter. A man will call you if he likes you enough, and if he believes you like him.

Other Reasons Men Call: Some Words of Caution

We encourage women to give men they like some positive reinforcement. We say this because we know it works! We are *not* saying that a woman should start having too many expectations. A woman should practice caution in the beginning of a relationship. She doesn't really know the man yet. All too often, we have seen that when a man calls a woman, it gives her a false sense of security. If she is interested in him, she lets her emotional guard down and begins to think that this guy really likes her. But he has just taken the first step, and she has no idea what his intentions are. All of a sudden, maybe a few weeks or months later, when he is nowhere to be found, she is left feeling hurt and rejected because she allowed herself to fall too hard too fast.

Certainly, there are men out there who will call women because they are in a position to begin a relationship and they are at a stage in their lives when they are ready to consider settling down. Unfortunately, this is the exception, not the rule.

Most guys will call for other reasons. The way we see it, finding the right girl is like finding a needle in a haystack. And we're going to need to make a lot of hay before we find her. Often we know right away that this girl is not the one for us. We may enjoy having her in our life to spend time with on a casual basis, on a Sunday night or on a weeknight when nothing better is happening. We enjoy the conversation and companionship but do not intend to get serious. There are other guys out there who will pursue a woman and call her because they have a special occasion coming up soon and need a date. Again, they have no intention of getting serious.

Finally, there are men out there who are players and call women just to have another one on their list. It sounds ugly, but it's true that some guys need to have many women in their lives to prove their manhood. In these cases, the guy does have a long-term plan, but it is not the one you think it is. His intention is to score. The more women he can sleep with, the more macho he'll be. This kind of man doesn't love women for who they are, but for what they can do for him. He doesn't care about seeing a woman's inner beauty. He is not interested in intimacy. He has little regard for her feelings or her body. All he is out to do is get laid.

We will discuss in the next chapter some of the signs you can look for that will serve as a warning when you are being played by a guy like this. But for now, a few words of caution. If a man is calling you, try to find out his real intentions. Get to know him. Don't settle for someone or some situation you don't really want. Don't fall prey to a guy who is not out for the same thing you are, and don't talk yourself into thinking he is when you know deep down inside that he isn't. This will save you time, heartache, and an unnecessary battering of your self-esteem.

Getting the Timing Right: How He Decides When to Call

Men understand that timing is essential and that the decision of when to call a woman for the first time is crucial. It is this very dilemma that gives men such trouble. We are constantly asking ourselves, "Should I call tomorrow or will I look like I am desperate? If I wait too long, will she think I am not interested?" Ultimately, this dilemma often forces men to take the easy way out and not call at all. Take it from us, we are speaking from personal experience and from countless discussions with other men. The first call is almost as difficult for us as is approaching a woman for the first time, if not more difficult.

This may sound like men playing games. After all, if we want to call, we should just call. The truth is, it is not a game. It is a defense mechanism men use to keep their vulnerability at a minimum. We don't want to look like saps, yet we don't want to lose a good thing.

Chris once spotted a girl on the beach that he had met at a party the night before. It was a hot and humid Sunday and everyone on the beach seemed to be hungover from the big party that had been thrown the previous night. They wound up throwing a Frisbee around for a while and taking a walk down to the water to cool off from the hot sand and the hot sun. Everything appeared to be going quite well. Chris got a lot of positive signals, including talking about going out together during the week. Sounds perfect, right?

Well, here is how it played out. Chris asked the woman for her phone number and she obliged. He was very confident that his phone call would be well received and he had really enjoyed her company. After a long day at work on Monday and a quick workout at the gym, Chris decided to give her a call. She answered the phone and sounded quite surprised to hear from him. Not surprised in a good way, though, and Chris sensed this immediately. The conversation was like a conversation from hell, filled with long silences that were often broken by stupid lines to break the silence.

In an effort to end this nightmare, Chris went ahead and asked her to get together one night during the week. He figured maybe she was just tired or had had a terrible day at work. She came up with one excuse after another and the conversation ended without any plan to get together. As Chris later found out, she thought that he was either desperate or was coming on too strong too fast. She couldn't figure out why they had spent time together Saturday night at the party and Sunday on the beach AND he had had to call her Monday night. She thought he had nothing else going on in his life and was turned off by that.

Just so you know: This is why men don't like to call too soon. We are afraid of looking desperate or like saps.

Brad was in a similar situation with different results. He met a woman through a coworker when she stopped by Brad's office to visit her friend and have lunch. Brad was invited along, and he hit it off with his coworker's friend right from the start. He was extremely interested in spending more time with her in an effort to get to know her better. Before she left to go back to work, he asked her if she would be interested in seeing him again and she said yes. They exchanged phone numbers and planned to talk later that week. Aware of what had happened to Chris, Brad decided to wait a couple of days before calling her.

Well, this was his biggest mistake. When he called her, she was not very receptive. She gave Brad one-word short answers and really didn't appear to be too interested in talking to him. Brad picked up on this negative vibe and politely ended the conversation. When he went to work the next day, he asked his coworker what was wrong with her friend. Brad was surprised to find out that she had been interested in him, yet he had waited too long to call her. This led her to believe that he was probably dating other women or that he wasn't very interested in her. She thought that if he wasn't dating anyone else, and he was interested in her, he should have called her much sooner. This gave her a bad impression, and she decided he was not the type of guy with whom she wanted to get involved.

So there you have it. These two scenarios show why it's so difficult for a man to decide how soon to call a woman he's just met and liked. We want to strike the right note by calling at the right time, not too soon and not too late.

But let's get something straight. A man may debate with himself over whether to call you the very next day, or within two or three days, but there is one thing we know for certain: *If we like a woman, we will call her within a week—and most likely in the next two or three days.*

Understand how a man's mind works. If a man doesn't call you within the first week, forget him. There's no potential for a relationship there. If he finally does call you, watch out! Suspect the worst. Feel free to imagine him at the other end of the line frantically trying to get something rolling. He's pooling all the random numbers in his wallet. He may have had a fight with his girlfriend, or he may have just broken up with her. Either way, he's only out looking for sex and a good time, not a meaningful relationship.

When he called more than a week later, did he ask if you had a friend to bring along for a double date? That means his buddy is in town. They are looking for sex. We hope you are listening carefully, because in our experience, women are too gullible when they agree to go out with a guy who called two weeks after first meeting her. If he's calling you more than a week later, he's up to no good. If he was really interested in you, he would have called you sooner.

Please Leave a Message at the Beep:
The Answering Machine Dilemma

By our definition, the first phone call means actually getting in touch with the woman, not her answering machine or her roommate. Most men will prefer *not* to leave a message on an answering machine or with a roommate when making the first call. Men won't leave a message because we don't want to give a woman the opportunity to not call back. That would hurt and would force us to make up some grand excuse to ourselves and our friends, like "The answering machine probably didn't work" or "Her roommate probably didn't give her the message."

To complicate matters, there are some women who feel they shouldn't have to return a man's phone call. They believe that *if he is really interested, he will call again*. This means that if a woman doesn't return his call in a timely way, a man will have to worry about the issue. Should he give a woman the benefit of the doubt and call her again? It's better not to leave a message so there is no chance the call will go unreturned.

So, if a man doesn't get in touch with you right away, he may have been trying to reach you but hasn't left a message. Or he may be delaying the call for a few days in order not to appear desperate. Give it some time and see what he has to say when he finally does reach you. You might even consider providing a man with your phone number at work. If you have a business card, give him one. The man is assured of reaching you. And the phone call is usually short, sweet, and to the point so that you avoid those uncomfortable silences and stupid lines that usually occur during that first telephone conversation.

When a man does take the risk and leaves a woman a message, this should be her most convincing signal that he is interested. And from a man's point of view, there is only one appropriate response from a woman interested in dating him. She must call him back. If she does not return his call, he will probably not call her again.

This is every man's worst nightmare come true. He has broken his own rule of not leaving a message. His ultimate fear of rejection by a woman has come to fruition. Right away, he will think he's inadequate. To avoid this humiliation, a man will play the macho role and refrain from calling again, even if he really wants to. There is no reason to open himself up to the same unbearable outcome. No matter how much a man is interested, if you do not return his first call, it is unlikely that he will call you again.

We do understand that it may be difficult for some women to do this. Some women may be shy, others old-fashioned. Some women may have *rules* that say they are not to call a man back. In these cases, it may be better for a woman to call a man at home during the day when he's at work. This is an opportune time to leave *him* a message to let him know that you returned his phone call and that you are interested. The ball is now back in his court. A return phone call to the man's answering machine is more than adequate encouragement for a professional man to continue to call a woman in whom he is interested.

For the women who have had a change of heart and regret having given out their phone numbers, or who have recently gotten back together with the ex-boyfriend, use your answering machine to your benefit. Screen, screen, screen. Men aren't stupid. Everyone is home at some point. The man will get the idea: He won't call you again.

Take the Initiative: Call Him

There is one point we would like to mention before moving on. There are women who do feel uncomfortable about giving out their phone numbers. These women often feel more comfortable in taking the man's phone number. As we've said, when a woman asks for a man's telephone number as an alternative to giving hers, men are usually convinced she will not call. Men understand the fears and uncertainty that surround that first call. So a man is usually very impressed with a woman who calls him first. It proves that you are a woman who is out to work for what she wants and will usually get it.

A common misconception held by women is that a man will lose respect for a woman who calls a man first. This is not true. Men appreciate women who take the initiative in the relationship. Calling a man first after the initial meeting can score major points.

But the timing of your call is as crucial as the timing of ours. If you are going to call him, you should do so in a timely way. If a woman calls a man a week, two weeks, or a month down the road, one result will probably be the same as calling him the next day or the day after meeting him. She will accomplish her goal of getting a date. However, if it takes you this long, his intentions will now have changed. He will suspect that you are not really interested, but are out to get something from him. He will think, If she really liked me, she would have called sooner. She must want to sleep with me. He will now think that he too will go out and try to get all he can. Typically, he will be asking himself, Why not go out with her; what do I have to lose? The idea that has entered his mind is that he is not going out on a date with a woman with whom he could start a relationship. Unless you are a woman who is looking for a casual, sexual relationship, we do not recommend this approach.

If you do call a man, he should seize the opportunity immediately and run with it. All you really need to say is something like, "Hi, it's Mary, we met last Friday night, and I said I would call." By his response, you will find out if he wants to pursue you. There is no need to ask him for a date. In fact, don't. Some men will say yes out of politeness, and that will waste your time. Other men will read into your invitation a note of desperation and be turned off. Best to just initiate the call and hear his response. If he responds in a lackluster way, end the conversation quickly and that will be that. If he responds with enthusiasm, he will ask you out in a matter of seconds or minutes.

Let's Get Together:
Asking for the First Date

Inevitably, if the will is there, the man and woman do manage to make the connection. After cutting through answering machines, paging services, roommates, work, workouts, self-doubt, and telephone tag, eventually you speak. In a man's mind, the first phone call serves one very specific purpose: setting up the first date.

If a woman is interested in dating this new man, she should do everything she can to take that first phone call. If for some reason she cannot, she should let the man know she is definitely going to call him back. Men are usually nervously waiting for that call to be returned. We want to avoid, at all costs, that empty feeling that accompanies rejection by a woman. An hour can seem like a day. If a woman does not return the call, as we stated before, it is a sure bet the man will not call back.

Since getting to know you is better in person, in-depth conversations should be left for the first date. When we have broken this rule, we have almost always regretted it. Long, rambling conversations do tend to occur during that first phone call before a blind date. Then we meet the girl, and there's no chemistry. We feel foolish for having spoken about too much too soon. We feel weird when we've told our life story to a complete stranger.

We recommend that the first phone call be brief, but we do recognize the need for some small talk. We appreciate it when women respond with enthusiasm to our questions and ask us questions too. There is almost no bigger turnoff during that first phone conversation than having a woman not be responsive or not reciprocate when asked a question. Men look for this signal because it generally means that she is not interested, or that she is dull, uneducated, or a lousy conversationalist. This kind of unresponsiveness will lead professional men to have second thoughts about dating the woman on the other end of the line. Ultimately, the professional man will not ask this type of woman out, and the relationship will have seen its final moments right there on the phone.

If a man does not ask a woman out on the first phone call, it should be the first sign that something is wrong. The chances are that something did not click during the conversation. If he says that he will call you back next week, his intentions are not good: He is stringing you along. If he makes no mention of calling you or seeing you, then you can be sure that that is the last time you'll hear from him.

When things do click between a man and a woman during that first phone call, he gets to the point soon enough. He will ask if you would like to get together, and you will say yes. Since the two of you lead busy lives, each of you will be reasonably flexible about where and when you will meet again. You will have refreshed that magic feeling sparked during your first encounter. You will experience that exhilarating feeling of anticipation. The two of you have now smoothed the way to an enjoyable first date.

Five

THE FIRST DATE

We'll leave it to women to tell us the stupid things men do on first dates. We are sure there are many! What we'll do is tell you of some common mistakes a woman makes when out with a guy for the first time. We'll also show you some surefire ways to win a man's heart right from the very beginning of the relationship. Once you stop making those mistakes, and start doing those things men love, you'll be sure to nab any man you want the first time you're out with him. You're going to be surprised by how easy it is! Men are much less complicated than women. Men can be pleased quite easily once you know what we want.

Men and women should make the most of a first date and not alienate each other for stupid reasons. Think about it: Many first dates never even happen! The statistical probability of meeting a woman, calling her, setting up a first date, and then actually going out is quite low. A professional man may call only 20 percent of the numbers he gets from women. Of those calls, he may continually get the answering machine or play phone tag one too many times. If and when he does get through to speak to her, she may turn him down and say something like, "Sorry, I was drunk when I gave you my number; I've got a boyfriend." Or the date may be broken and never be rescheduled because she is busy, he is busy, and nobody has anything invested yet. The chances of that first date actually taking place are slim. We say this not to be bleak, but to emphasize how random and chancey meeting the man of your dreams and igniting a relationship with him can be. Even when the spark is there, it can quickly be smothered. Many first dates are last dates because men and women unwittingly alienate each other.

Will It Be a Dream Date or a Nightmare?

On a first date, a woman may capture a man's interest and make him eager to see her again. Or she may make a man want to say "Check, please" and run for the hills. Let's face it: There is often a fine line between a first date that turns into a last date or one that evolves into a serious relationship. A woman and a man may be right for each other, but something trivial gets in the way and they never pursue a relationship. What we want to talk about here are those first dates that could have been great but were not. What turns a potential dream date into a nightmare?

We have thought long and hard about those first-date experiences we have had that were pleasurable and those that were nightmares. What topped the list for making a first date a nightmare—besides zero chemistry—was when we felt awkward or uncomfortable about *how* we talked and *what* we talked about. Monologues are not fun. Everyone likes a date who is intelligent and responsive. If a woman does not listen or pose questions, or wishes only to tell her own story, a man will find her needy, dull, and impolite. And *what* she talks about could mean the difference between a man asking for a second date or jumping ship.

The Nightmare Date:
She Won't Stop Talking About the Ex

When a woman dwells too long on the topic of her ex-boyfriend, a man feels discouraged. If it was a recent breakup, a man can understand that an ex-boyfriend is on her mind. He will also know that she is not ready for a relationship with him. He will worry that she will always compare him to the ex-boyfriend. He will think, There is no possible way I can compete with this guy. He probably shared some great times with her. When a man feels too discouraged, he loses interest.

If she boasts about how handsome or rich or smart her ex is, her date will feel annoyed. She's boasting, she's insecure, he'll think. Don't think that being the object of some other guy's desire will make you more valuable in this man's eyes. He may just see that you are trying desperately to impress him. He'll see your insecurity.

When women catalogue their ex-boyfriend's faults, inevitably men think about her shortcomings, not the ex-boyfriend's. When she says, "He cheated on me; I don't know why I stayed with him," he thinks, She's a pushover. When she says, "I didn't really care about him, but I stayed with him out of pity," he thinks, She's a martyr. When a woman picks on her ex-boyfriend, a man will take it as a warning: If I stick around, she'll do that to me someday.

Men also worry that a woman who dwells too much on the ex-boyfriend is unstable. Men wonder why women go back to their exes. Women say, "I needed to find out for sure. Going back to him reinforced my feeling that I didn't want him anymore. Now I know that I will never go back to him." Men think, Of course you won't . . . until the next time. Please do not misunderstand us. We do know that it is hard to sever ties with someone you love or loved. Breaking off with the wrong guy requires extreme self-confidence, motivation, and maturity. We cannot even count the women we know with ex-boyfriends who are in and out of their lives. Something is missing in that relationship, but she just cannot seem to sever the ties. If it did not work out once or even twice, why would a woman go back? The only logical answer, unless she is a masochist and enjoys emotionally painful relationships, is that she is insecure, unstable, and unable to move on with her life without him.

Talking about the ex defeats the purpose of the date, which is to get to know each other. Because of this, men are unlikely to talk about their ex-girlfriends on the first date. Even if it is a fresh breakup and his ex-girlfriend is still on his mind, he is on a date with another woman and is attempting to move on with his life. He is trying to get to know the woman he is with. He cannot possibly do that if he is talking about his ex-girlfriend. When a woman talks about her ex, men ask themselves, How is she attempting to get to know me?

With the possible exception of her saying, "I ended it and didn't look back," a man is not interested in hearing about the ex on a first date. So, if you want him to ask you out for a second date, avoid the subject of your ex. Concentrate on connecting with the man in front of you.

The Nightmare Date:
She Delves into Serious Topics Too Soon

Women tend to be more verbal than men, but eloquence may miss the mark when too much is spoken too soon. We say this because so many women try to win us with words. Instead of words bringing us closer, they often set us adrift from each other. We are suspicious of women who wish to become too intimate too soon.

Talking about serious topics, such as prior abusive relationships or a bad family history, will throw a man into a tailspin. If a woman starts talking about her parents' divorce, or her brother's drug problem, or her grandmother's recent death, how is a man supposed to react? If she confesses that she has an eating disorder and is on antidepressants, what is a man supposed to say? It is difficult for a man to know how to react to these confidences. We feel compassion, but we don't know how to respond appropriately because we don't know her very well. He wonders, Does she want advice? Does she want me to comfort her? He is being called upon to do something he is not prepared to do. Delving into topics that are too serious on the first date will make a man feel awkward and uncomfortable. Couples need to have in-depth conversations about tough issues, but the first date is not the right occasion for this.

In the same way, future goals and aspirations are fine topics for discussion, but a man does not like to talk about plans for marriage and children on the first date. Save these topics for later in the relationship. There is nothing wrong with taking it slowly and letting things progress naturally. It has been our experience that the better, longer-lasting relationships were the ones in which these deeper topics were not discussed early on, when the two people didn't really know each other. Good relationships, instead, seemed to move ahead on "cruise control." The relationships that ended the most quickly were the ones in which the woman continuously talked about "wanting more," moving to the next level, settling down, and planning for the future. We know so many women who scared off great guys because of their inability to just "go with the flow" and allow things to progress naturally.

What is appropriate conversation when you are trying to get to know a stranger? Since first impressions are hard to erase, and you don't know the guy, we advise discretion. Remember: The man and woman do not know each other very well and they are usually judging every word that is spoken. You don't want to be misjudged. Rich will never forget one first date that, for him, was over before it had begun. He and his date were driving to the restaurant when his car was cut off by another driver. At the next traffic light, the girl rolled down her window and shouted obscenities at the other driver. Imagine what Rich thought when his date yelled, "You goddamn motherfucking bastard." No second date that time.

Like talking about the ex, and delving into serious topics too soon, using obscenities is just going too far on a first date. Some people let their guard down too fast and try to force intimacy. Others remain too guarded, too shy, too distant. On a dream date, a man and a woman manage to strike the balance—and *relax*.

The Dream Date: She's . . . Nice!

Women are astonished when we tell them what many professional men look for in a woman on the first date—besides chemistry, of course. Are you ready to hear what men hope to find in a woman they are dating for the first time? Men like women who are nice. Men are suckers for kindness and consideration. We love women who are affable, flexible, easygoing. Most men cannot resist a sweet woman.

Of course, we don't mean a woman should be so flexible that it appears she doesn't have a life, or so eager to please that she risks becoming a doormat. We are just saying that it is important to be nice. We have dated many women who tried hard to be brilliant, sexy, and challenging when, really, all we wanted them to do was be comfortable, relaxed, and themselves.

Because when she is relaxed, then we can be relaxed too. And when we are at ease, then we can be our best self.

Understand how a man usually feels on a first date: We are worried that the drinks aren't cold enough, that the food won't be good enough. We worry that she doesn't like our choice of restaurant, or that she doesn't like us. First dates are inherently stressful, and so we are relieved when a woman has enough grace to take the anxious edge off the evening.

When he is on a first date, a professional man often feels the pressure to perform. It is as if we were actors in a Broadway show, doing evening shows and matinees. We've got to impress the audience and get a good review in the *New York Times*. Sometimes we try so hard we feel like a clown in a circus. We've got to put on the nose, pitch the tent, crack jokes, and dance around. We get tired of putting on an act. Imagine our relief when she says, "I don't care what we do, let's just relax and have a good time."

Do you hear what we are saying? We are saying that the girl who eases the tension fastest wins the race. Every guy feels this way. *Don't believe that being hard to please or myste-*

riously distant wins a man's affection. It's just not true. Do something affirmative instead of taking that step backward so many women take. When a woman acts too mysterious or too distant, a guy feels as if she is making him run through a forest in the dark. Very often we think to ourselves, Better get out of this forest now, while I still know the route out!

We can't tell you how relieved and happy we feel when we're out on a date with a woman who says things like, "I had such a bad day at work, but it's so great to be here and to be here with you. You know what? This restaurant is fabulous! I've never been here before; how in the world did you find out about this place?" If a woman expresses pleasure, we immediately begin to loosen up and start talking seriously to her. And while we begin formulating questions to find out more about her and start to tell her what's on our minds, a little voice inside our head whispers, What a great girl! Ask her for the second date during dessert.

Anatomy of a First Date: Figuring Out the Game Plan

A professional man knows that chivalry is not dead. He firmly believes that he should be the one to ask the woman out on a first date. He also feels it is his duty to plan it. This can be a difficult task, especially when he doesn't know a woman too well and doesn't know what she likes to do. We try very hard to plan something she will enjoy.

If a guy goes to the trouble of planning all of the details of the date, it is not a great idea to shoot him down and tell him that you hate his plan. We remember when Brad orchestrated a night on the town with a woman he had just met and liked. He called a very fancy restaurant well in advance, made reservations, and told the woman a few days before what time to be ready and where they were going. To his surprise, she responded with an adamant, "I don't want to go there; how about going to this place on the other side of town?" Brad felt totally shot down, which led him to resent her and feel that she was not the girl for him. That relationship did not progress very far.

Just to show how difficult it is for a man to plan a first date with a woman he barely knows, we can tell you that all of us at one point or another thought it would be best just to pick a night and a time. Once that was accomplished, we would then ask the woman, "Well, what do you want to do?" Often the response was, "I don't know, what do you want to do?" We were then left to wonder, Should we ask her out for drinks or would she like to go out to dinner? If she thinks dinner is okay, what type of food does she like? Will she be impressed with my choice of restaurant, or will she think I am cheap if the restaurant is not to her liking? Does it even matter to her? As you can see, deciding the game plan for the first date is not as simple as it sounds. We tend to think that cosy, intimate, unpretentious places are best for first dates—somewhere with a warm, relaxing atmosphere. Stiff, fussy places should be avoided. And it does help if you provide us with some subtle hints regarding where you would like to go.

Restaurants allow for conversation and can be a good place to get to know each other. Sometimes, for a couple out for the first time, a restaurant can be uncomfortable. It can be awkward to eat in front of someone you don't know. If the service isn't good, the man feels pressured to complain to the waiter to ensure that everything is going smoothly and that the woman is enjoying herself. A lot can go wrong that can prove to be embarrassing and stressful. More often than not, though, we tend to fall back on dinner as the "old reliable."

Lounges and coffee bars are good alternatives to restaurants, and may be more conducive to a man and a woman getting to know each other. The uneasy feeling of eating in front of someone you barely know is not there, and you can sit close together and engage in meaningful conversation. When you can relax, you can be yourself, and when you can be yourself, you have a better shot at getting to know each other for who you really are. This is a good thing, because you may find out sooner rather than later that you really are compatible, or you may find that you can't stand this guy and want to run for the hills.

Movies are not a great first-date choice. How can sitting in a dark room surrounded by hundreds of people, listening to the articulate Sly Stallone and the witty Arnold Schwarzenegger, allow the man and the woman to get to know each other? He may have planned this because he is shy; the movie theater is a safe haven for him. He does not have to worry about conversation if he is in a movie theater. He may also have planned this date because he is cheap. Going to the movies is much cheaper than going out for dinner or drinks. Or, he may have planned this date because he has a girlfriend. He may feel that being in a movie theater is a safe place because he will not be seen in public with another woman. A man with any of these characteristics is not the professional man for you.

Unlike movies, museums and art exhibits do allow time for conversation. If a man asks a woman to go on a date to one of these places, he is interested in getting to know her. It also shows that he is somewhat cultured and may be looking to see if the woman is as well. Men who suggest these places could be good candidates for being "Mr. Right."

We will admit, though, that a professional man will often feel pressured to impress a woman on a first date. There are many ways to impress a woman, but, unfortunately, the need to impress often translates into spending money. Men are trained to feel that if we don't take a woman out to a nice restaurant, we won't make the first round of cuts. We can't tell you how many stories we have heard, from our female friends and from women we have dated, about women who boasted about the fancy restaurants they had been taken to on dates. It seems as if it is some type of competition between women. A typical dialogue may proceed like this: "Do you believe John took me to Sign of the Dove on Tuesday night? I was so impressed." Her friend would respond by saying, "Really, that is very impressive, he has great taste. But guess what? Joe took me to Le Cirque last Wednesday. I thought that was so thoughtful of him, especially on our first date. He really scored a lot of points in my book." Honestly, these are true stories. It makes us sick to our stomachs to believe that women put so much emphasis on where they are taken out to eat on the first date.

Is the purpose of the first date to see how much money a man will drop on you? Is the purpose of a first date to get something to eat? Or is the purpose of the first date to get to know the man better? Men like to spend time with "the guys" because of their laid-back, flexible natures. We look for this quality in a woman. Do you feel comfortable telling your friends that the man of your dreams took you to a coffee bar on the first date and maybe spent a total of ten dollars on you? Come on, now, be honest.

The truth is that *a man wants to be liked for himself, not for what he will spend on you or do for you*. In guy terms, a woman who appreciates this—a woman with positive energy and affability—is a "cool chick." Please don't take offense at the use of the word "chick." It is just a guy thing, and a word that guys use among other guys. When a man tells his friends that you are a "cool chick," this is considered a great compliment. If you have no problem with going to a coffee bar or a lounge on the first date, you are on your way to being a "cool chick." However, if going to the best restaurant in town is on your mind, just so you can brag to your friends about where you went, or if you judge a man by how much money he spends on the first date, the chances are that you haven't yet achieved "cool chick" status.

Go with the Flow— Yes, Even on a Work Night

There are often times when a woman has ended a perfectly good date too early because she is paranoid that she won't be able to get up for work the next day, or might even turn into a pumpkin. When this happens, a man will always think she is not interested in him, no matter how well the date went. If a woman must end the date early but did have a good time, it is important for her to tell the man that she had a good time. Here's how a woman might finesse this difficult moment:

WOMAN: Remember when we first set up this date, I told you I'd have to end the evening early? I'm having such a great time, I'm sorry I have to go so soon. But I have a big presentation tomorrow. I know you know what that's like.

MAN: Yeah, I understand. May I call you again?

WOMAN: Absolutely. I'd love to go out with you again.

Telling him she had a good time gives him a reason, and the incentive, to call again, sooner rather than later.

However, if circumstances are not really pressing, and the date is going well, why end it early? If it is a weeknight, we all know that both the man and the woman have to get up early for work the next day. It is appealing to a man when a woman will make the extra effort to stay out a little later. Sure, it is a little painful when that annoying buzzer goes off at 6:00 A.M. and you had only four hours of sleep, but if you are having fun, suck it up. You'll make it through the day (riding the high you get from a good first date), and then you can go home and take a little catnap.

"Check Please":
Payment Etiquette on the First Date

We reiterate: Chivalry is not dead. If a man asks a woman out on a date, he should pay—no ifs, ands, or buts. It is a nice gesture for a woman to offer to pay, but a professional man will decline. May we suggest that if the penny-pincher sitting across from you on the first date accepts your offer to pay, think twice about seeing him again. Where was this guy brought up, in a cave? If you feel you must offer as a polite gesture, you will surely score points, but if you argue about it and insist, you will lose those points just as quickly. Professional men like to get the bill paid without its becoming an issue. So sit back and relax. This one is on us.

If the date gets expensive, for instance, if there is dinner, drinks elsewhere, and a few rounds of cab fare, it is a nice gesture if a woman pays for a small part of the date. A man will not feel insulted. When a woman offers to pay, it is a sign that she is sophisticated, independent, and generous. A professional man seeks a woman who possesses characteristics such as these. We have heard that some women think it is insulting to a man to offer him money if the bills are piling up on the first date. If a woman has any reservations about offering to pay, she should know that it's not insulting. This shows a man that the relationship is not going to be a one-way street. It shows that the woman isn't petty about money, an important part of a first impression. He will tell his friends that he thought you were cool because you offered to pay.

If a woman insists on "going Dutch," splitting the bill, we assume she has discovered that she does not like us. Yes, we have had this experience. She is not into us and feels she doesn't want to be in the position of "owing us anything." If you like the guy, don't insist. Show your independent spirit by putting your money away and saying, "The next one's on me."

All you really need to do is say, "Thank you." With these words, a woman shows her appreciation. Without them, a man feels she is taking advantage of him. Believe it or not, we have all been on first dates where we have gone to the wallet for the entire night and our date never thanked us. Remember: *Men always need to be reassured that they are being appreciated.*

"Would You Like to Go Out Again?": Be Prepared for a Second-Date Request

If the date has gone well, it is likely that the man will ask the woman for a second date. This question could come at any time during the date, so be prepared. By requesting a second date, he indicates his interest. A man also uses this question to find out how the woman is feeling about him. Don't be surprised if a man asks you to go out the very next day. Men like spontaneous women, and we don't like to feel that we have to plan every move we make.

If you like him, there is no reason to hide it or try to get the upper hand. Forget playing hard to get. Playing games like this one does not make a man chase a woman harder. It only causes a man to become frustrated and not pursue you further. A professional man does not have time for this. Think about it. Why make a man who has already declared his interest chase you? The more likely outcome of your actions will be that he thinks you weren't interested in him, his innate insecurity will take over, and he will talk himself right out of wanting to see you again. If fear of rejection does not scare him away, then the feeling of having to chase you will. We figure, "Why should I chase her when I already made it clear that I would like to see her again?"

What He Means When He Says "I'll Call You"

If a man says the infamous words "I'll call you" as he is walking away from your front doorstep, he is usually just saying this to ease the uncomfortable feeling of ending. This comment has *no* meaning. Women should not try to decipher it or harp on it. Just pretend you did not hear it. So many of our female friends put so much emphasis on this phrase and make themselves crazy when, in fact, it doesn't mean anything. They say to themselves or their friends, "He said he would call me, which either means he likes me and will call, or he may not like me and won't call, or maybe he isn't sure. . . ." Please, do not beat yourself up over this phrase. It means nothing. It's filler, something to say as he walks away, leaving all options open.

The End of the First Date:
Should You Invite Him In? Or Kiss Him?

We do not recommend inviting a man into your house after
the first date, nor do we recommend going to his house. If
you do, a lot can go wrong that may ruin the potential for a
relationship. Many thoughts enter a man's mind if a woman
invites him in or if she is willing to go back to his place. A
woman can never go wrong by kissing a man good night
and going her separate way. No man wants to think the
woman of his dreams is promiscuous. So put the hormones
to rest and just let it be. There will be plenty of time for the
good stuff later on.

For now, you have the first kiss to look forward to. He
understands that it is up to him to make the move for the
kiss good night. Will it be a pleasurable moment or an awkward one? It may not even happen. Even if the date went
well, it is still a difficult move for us to make. A man thinks,
Should I kiss her or shouldn't I? Should I French-kiss her or
just settle for a peck on the lips? How will she respond? Will
she kiss me back? Will she French-kiss me back? Will she
turn and offer her cheek? Or will she just offer a simple
handshake? If a man gives a woman a peck on the cheek, it
can mean one of two things. He either did not like her, or he
is too shy and passive. If he tries to kiss her and she shirks it,
he will feel humiliated.

A good-night kiss on the lips, well given and well received,
is the perfect end to the first date.

Six

So Far, So Good:
The Follow-Up

The First Date Was So Enjoyable . . .

So far, so good. You just got home from your first date with
an exciting new guy. You think the date went well. He was
smart, handsome, and he made you laugh. All evening, he
showed an interest in what you had to say. Even though you
have known him for less than twenty-four hours, you feel
close to him and very attracted to him. Toward the end of
the date, the two of you playfully flirted with each other and
you really wanted to tear his clothes off and make passionate
love to him, but you kept your cool and kissed him instead.
He said he would call you. An hour later, still dancing on air,
you are on the phone with your best friend telling her all the
details. You can't wait to hear his voice again. For the next
two nights, you stay home purposely in order not to miss his
call. Then the unthinkable happens. There is no call, no

message, not even a quick ring and a hang-up. Nothing. For the next couple of weeks you ask yourself the same question over and over again: Why didn't he call?

Why Didn't He Call Me Again?

Almost every woman asks herself this question after a first date at least once in her life. It is puzzling, even maddening, when you have a good first date with a man you like and he fails to call you again. The truth is that a couple on a date may be in the same place at the same time but be having completely different experiences. The woman may think she is opening herself up and bonding with him on a deep issue. Meanwhile, he is thinking, Uh-oh, here we go again, the ex-boyfriend. Or the woman may think she is being suitably cool and distant. Meanwhile, he fears she doesn't like him. Men and women often misinterpret each other and so proceed to disconnect. Why wouldn't he call? Here's why.

You May Have Sent the Wrong Signals

After the first date, if a man liked you, he will want to set up a second date and see you again. Before he calls you, he will think back on the time you spent together and scrutinize any negative signals. His mental scale goes into action. He enters the same mode he was in before he dialed your number for the first time, only now he has much more information to digest. Should I call her again? Does she like me? To calm his insecurity, he must assure himself that you want to see him again. If a man has even the slightest suspicion that you did not like him, his mental scale will be tipped to the negative side and he will not call you. He does not want to give you the opportunity to reject him.

Since every man is inherently insecure, he *will definitely* pick up on any negative vibes that you are giving off. He may even misconstrue inconsequential things you say or do as negative signals.

Chris was on a date with a woman he met one day in the park. Before the date, they spoke on the phone a number of times and had great conversations. Both were very excited about their first date, which was dinner at a small, quiet restaurant. To Chris's surprise, she was not at all talkative during dinner. In fact, she was downright silent. Chris tried to carry the conversation, but there was no hope. During those long uncomfortable pauses, he was squirming in his seat, just waiting to get out of there. He could not believe the change in her: The woman who had been so open and talkative with him on the phone was so quiet in person.

What was wrong? The moment it occurred to him that she might not want to be there with him, he made the decision to end the date as quickly as possible and never call her again. At the end of the date, she apologized for being so quiet, explaining that she was tired after an unexpectedly long day at work. Chris rethought his decision and considered calling her again, but the damage had been done. His mental scale was stuck on the negative side, and he never called.

It's important to be responsive and animated on a first date—even if you are tired. Everyone is tired, especially hardworking professionals. But we try to get over it and get with it!

Brad had a similar experience with a woman he had had a good first date with. For their second date, he invited her out on a double date with his law partner and the partner's girlfriend. It was a night that could have been memorable. They were at a great restaurant where they knew the chef personally. Food was being piled on the table; the champagne was flowing. Brad's partner's date was witty and charming. Unfortunately, Brad's date didn't say a word during dinner. In fact, it seemed to him she was barely functioning. As she was getting up to leave early, she mentioned to him that she was a bit hungover from her night out the evening before. He thought to himself, I suppose she didn't care enough about our second date to avoid getting a hangover the night before. When she called him two months later, asking, "Why haven't you called?" he told her he had met someone else. He had met someone else, but that wasn't the reason he hadn't called her. He hadn't called her because she was a deadbeat date.

A professional man will pick up on all those negative signals. In general, any negative comments about the man or the date are a bad idea. This may seem obvious, but we say it here because we are astounded by how many women will criticize their dates about their jobs, clothes, beliefs, interests, or families. Any direct confrontations or hostile debates on the first date will ensure that a second date will not be any time soon.

Brad was on a date with a fellow lawyer he'd met at a party. It was election time and they were talking about campaign issues. Well, as luck would have it, they had opposite opinions about every topic they discussed. They wound up battling over everything from capital punishment to saving the whales. Brad likes to argue, so he was enjoying himself, but to him it seemed as if she were deliberately trying to contradict everything he said. He could not believe she was belittling his ideas and beliefs on their first date instead of trying to get to know him better. He never called her again.

Don't get us wrong, men love healthy—even heated—conversation and debate. We are not interested in a woman without a mind of her own who nods yes to everything we say. What we run from is a woman who seems less interested in getting to know us than in attacking who we are and what we do. We are sure women have their reasons for going into attack mode, but in terms of the do's and don'ts of dating, if you like the guy, don't attack him. He would rather swim in shark-infested waters than pick up the phone and talk to you again.

Far less than that will prevent him from dialing your number. Two things women do on dates always trigger a man's insecurities. The first is ending the date early. As we've said, no matter what reason a woman gives—"I have to get up early for work," or "There's a great ABC movie of the week I don't want to miss," or "I have to get my nails done"— it all means one thing to a man: She is not interested. A man wants to feel that he's special enough for you to sacrifice a little in order to spend some time with him. Making room for him in your hectic schedule makes *him* want to please *you*.

If you really do have to end the date early, and you want him to call you again, tell him early in the date that you will have to cut it short. If you know you'll need to end the date early when the two of you set it up, you can even give him the option of rescheduling for another night. Giving him the option will short-circuit his natural tendency to believe you don't like him when you leave early.

WOMAN: Yes, I am free Tuesday night of this week. I do have an early flight out the next morning for a business trip, so it will need to be an early evening. We can do that or we can see each other the following week, whichever you prefer.

MAN: Let's see each other this Tuesday.

WOMAN: Great! I look forward to it.

The second thing a woman does that will trigger a man's insecurity is to shrug her shoulders and be noncommittal when he refers to doing things together in the future. He is definitely interested in you and testing the waters for your interest in a second date. He is giving you the opportunity to show him your interest. If he hears anything other than "Sure, I would like to go out with you again," you may never hear from him again, no matter how well the date went. Anything other than a positive answer is a tremendous blow for a man to take on a first date. He will have a tough time calling you again.

If You Like the Guy, Be Sure to Send the Right Signals

The message is, *If you want a man to call you again, you have to make sure he knows you are interested in him*. We are not suggesting you be overeager. There is no need to hit him with a barrage of fake-sounding compliments. He is simply looking for signals that show you are enjoying the date and are happy to be with him. A man needs his ego stroked. Showing interest in his life and career is a good starting point. A large part of a professional man's life is his career. He will always appreciate a woman who shows interest in his profession and wants to know more about it.

If you truly like your date, and you want him to know it, subtle signs of affection during the date will do the trick. *Positive body language will always work in your favor*. An innocent touch of his hand when he says something funny, or grasping his arm as you cross the street, will definitely let him know you like him and want to see him again. Using this subtle body contact during a date will greatly increase the chances of his calling again.

Speaking of body contact, we will say again that the good-bye kiss is a key moment. You may wish it never happened or you may remember it all your life. For a man, the kiss can make or break the date. When he thinks back on the date, he will remember that kiss. If he tries to kiss you and you turn your cheek or back off, he will think, She is not attracted to me, she did not have a good time, she doesn't like me. He will be less likely to call you again if this happens. There's no worse rejection than going for the lips and getting the cheek. On the other hand, it might be inappropriate for a guy to even try. He may not even attempt to kiss you if he thought the date did not go well. If you thought it did go well, a small kiss initiated by you and planted on his cheek may change his mind.

Be Proactive:
Call Him and Thank Him for a Great Date

Many women ask us if it is okay to call a man after the first date. The answer is absolutely YES! Men do like it when women call them, and after the first date is no exception. Forget the fear that he will perceive you as desperate. It is just not true. He will be incredibly happy to hear from you. This one simple call by you will put an end to any remaining doubts in his mind that you may not like him. He will also think more highly of you because it shows that you are appreciative of him and confident in yourself. These are two qualities that every professional man looks for in a woman. If you really want to charm him, saying "I'm just calling to thank you for last night" will do wonders. This is music to any man's ears. It lets him know that you had a good time with him and that you probably want to see him again. This will make him feel more confident in himself, and he will be more likely to ask you out for a second date (and probably a third and a fourth).

By calling him to thank him for a great first date, you have just placed a ton of weight on the positive side of his mental scale. You will also stand apart from the other women he has gone out with who have rarely called him, shown him no appreciation, and expected everything to be done for them. *He has been desperately waiting for a woman like you who will call him and just say thank you for the date.* You will make such an impression that this will immediately put you on the fast track to the "serious relationship." You will get more frequent calls from him, you will meet his parents more quickly, and *he will fall in love with you sooner.*

Rich and Marla decided to go ice-skating on their first date. He picked her up, and they were off to the brand-new outdoor rink by the waterfront. It was a brisk, sunny winter day and it seemed that everyone else had the same idea. The ice was packed with people. When they approached the counter to get skates, they saw a sign that said "Next available skating time at 4:00 P.M." Unfortunately, it was only one o'clock. Rich was then faced with a dilemma. He had no back-up plan. After an extremely awkward fifteen minutes of trying to figure out what to do, in an act of desperation, Rich suggested that they go to the aquarium conveniently located near the ice-skating rink.

In Rich's mind, this date was going downhill fast. After they arrived at the aquarium, Rich attempted to salvage the date by trying to get Marla to laugh at his dumb jokes about the funny-looking blowfish. Luckily, it worked. They became more relaxed and had a great time. The next thing they knew, it was time for dinner. Marla suggested a nice restaurant, and they had a very cozy, romantic dinner. They were so engrossed in their conversation that they did not realize it was one in the morning and the restaurant was closing. Unfortunately, it was time for the date to end. The next day, Marla left a message on Rich's answering machine just to say how much she'd enjoyed their date the night before. This made Marla stand out among all the other women Rich had dated. He was very happy to hear that she liked him, and he called her right back. They went out that night to the ballet on a whim and had another great date.

We must give you one word of caution about women calling men after the first date. Men do not like it when women constantly call them. This spells one thing in a man's mind—N-A-G. He will lose interest in you if you call him frequently, especially early on. One nice phone call after the date will set you on the right track, but a series of phone calls will have him running for the hills.

The bottom line is that *if you had a good time on the first date, and want to see him again, let him know*. Another helpful hint is to *call him once soon after the date, but not more*. If you do these simple things, the chances are that you will not be asking yourself, Why didn't he call?

He Called!

If you both like each other and you sent the right signals, he will call. And believe it or not, the follow-up phone call will still be awkward for him. Once again, it is because of his insecurity. He needs to know you had a good time with him and want to see him again. He will try to elicit more positive feedback from you to put himself at ease and give him the confidence to ask you for a second date. You can simplify this process by letting him know you enjoyed spending time *with him* on the date. Don't go overboard with the compliments. This will make him think that you are too interested and he may perceive you as desperate. One or two short, sweet comments will suffice. He will pick up on this, and you will reap the benefits.

How Interested Is He?

Once the tension of this second call has eased, the tone of the conversation can let you know how interested he is in you. Does he ask you about your job or your family? Has he remembered a lot about you and is he concerned about the important things in your life? Is he still trying to learn more about you as a person? If the answer to these questions is yes, then he thinks highly of you. The length of the conversation also indicates his interest. In general, if a professional man has a lengthy conversation on the phone with you, then he definitely likes you. This shows that he is giving up some of his busy day for you. He has begun to open his life to you.

On the other hand, if the calls that follow the date are short, superficial, and meaningless, then he is probably not interested in you. You may ask, "Then why is he calling me?" He is simply keeping his options open by staying in touch with you. He may be dating many women at the same time or may be in a relationship that is on the rocks. He may even be stringing you along in the hope that he will have sex with you at some point soon. These scenarios occur very frequently, and you should be aware of them. If a professional man is interested in you, he will take time out of his busy lifestyle to talk to you and get to know you better.

Sometimes a guy will call you again, you will have a great conversation with him, but he will not ask you out on a second date. This can mean two things. The first is that he is still not sure you are interested in him. If he is still insecure despite all your efforts, then he is probably just shy.

If he is not shy, then he is chatting you up. That means he probably either has another woman he is dating or is just stringing you along for sex. He will turn on the charm to keep you interested in him so that when he wants to go out with you at some later date, he can. This will cause you much frustration. You will constantly be asking yourself, What is this guy up to? It seems as if he likes me, but we just seem to be phone buddies.

In both of these situations, we say take the initiative and ask the guy out. If he hesitates at all in saying yes to a date, then he is playing games with you. He may truly like you, but he is not being fair to you. If you continue to play along with his games, then you will end up with heartache. You should forget this guy. On the other hand, if he says yes right away, he is probably just shy.

The timing of the phone call after the first date can also give you an indication of how interested he is in you. If the man does not call soon after the date, then he is not looking to start a serious relationship with you. *There is no way a man who is seriously interested in a woman would wait longer than two or three days to call.*

If he wants to see you again, he will do whatever it takes to get in touch with you. If he has meetings all day, he will try to give you a call at his lunch break. If he is leaving town for the next week, he will either tell you so before the end of your date or he will call you before he leaves. He may even call you while he is away. At the very least, he will leave a message on your answering machine saying that he will be out of town and will call you when he gets back.

So, if it takes a man a week or longer to call you after your first date, then forget him. He is probably dating several women and will be adding you to his list.

No-Win Situations

There are certain situations in which a man will definitely not call you—and you will be lucky if he doesn't. This type of man is either dating another woman, not ready for a relationship, or is simply not interested in you.

The man who is not interested in you is easy to spot. He sends definite signals that you should pick up on very easily. If a man does not like a woman, he will not pay attention to her on the date and will do whatever he can to end the date early. He will stop trying to impress the woman and will end his good-behavior routine. Sometimes he will be downright rude. He will look at every woman in the restaurant, hit on the waitress, and start talking about topics that disturb women. He will tell you how much of a womanizer he is and how he is not looking for a girlfriend right now. Other times he will be disrespectful of you in a charming way. He may jokingly jab at you with sarcastic comments. If you have been talking about the other men in your life, he might say: "How wonderful that so many guys like you; I wonder what they see." When the bill comes, he may—as a joke—refer to your paying for all of it, or for your share. He may make sexual innuendos about the waitress, you, or any other woman in the room. You may misconstrue this as playful kidding, but we know that no man would act this way (jokingly or not) in the presence of a woman with whom he wanted a relationship. Don't let his charm fool you, and be happy if you never hear from him again.

An acquaintance of ours went on a date with a woman who constantly complained about everything on the date. She let her opinions be known: The restaurant was too dark, the soup was cold, his job (as a biochemical engineer) was boring. Each word she uttered sent a chill down his spine. Each minute he spent with her was as painful as a red-hot poker being stuck in his eye. He was searching around the room for something that could divert his attention. To his relief and delight, a television at the bar in the restaurant was playing his favorite episode of *Baywatch*. He countered every negative comment she made about his car or dog or sports team with how lovely Pamela Anderson Lee's breasts looked and how tight her ass was. This is an extreme example, but it shows how rude men can become on a date when they don't like the woman.

Let us be absolutely honest and tell you the ugly truth about men. We say this guy looked at other women—real or televised—to divert his attention in order to escape from the woman he was with. But that's not all that was going on. In this case, this guy was not only seeking to escape his date's criticism, but to get back at her, to even the score.

Sometimes when a man is not interested in a woman, he will change the tone of his conversation and begin to talk in a sexually suggestive way. He will discuss sexual topics, hoping for a positive response so he can get some action. *He knows he does not like her but will still try to get sex from her*. If he does get sex, he will never call again. If he doesn't get sex, he may call again to get one more shot at getting laid.

Once again, though, after he gets laid he will not call again. *In general, if a guy is very open about sexual topics on the first date, he is not looking to build a relationship.*

The man who is dating another woman is more difficult to recognize. He is probably using you to confirm whether or not he loves the other woman. He may also be having trouble in his relationship. He decided to play the field and go out with you, but now realizes he really wants to be with the other woman after all. This man will rarely give you his phone number for fear you will call when his girlfriend is at his place. He will probably not ask you to go out on a weekend night because he reserves this night for his steady girlfriend. If you really do like this guy, but you are not sure if he has a girlfriend, force the issue by asking for his number and requesting a weekend date. If he balks for any reason, he is playing games with you and you should forget him.

Finally, there is the guy who is "not ready" for a relationship. He is classically the younger, good-looking stud who goes out scamming every week from Wednesday to Sunday. If he has not had sex in a while, he will set up a date with one of the many women he has met in the last few weeks. This is the type of guy who will put on the moves from the minute the date starts. He will be very sexual and will use all of the tricks in his book to get you turned on so much that you will go against your good sense and have sex with him. No doubt he will wine and dine you and you will have a great time with him. He has picked up many tricks from his vast experience with women. He knows what women like and what they want to hear. It will not matter if you have sex with him or not—he will not call you in the hope of starting a serious relationship. If you do sleep with him, he may call you back two weeks later or at 3:00 A.M. one night looking for sex. Obviously, if you are looking for a relationship, our advice is to stay away from this type of guy and be thankful if he never calls you again.

Your Goal:
Nurture Mr. Right, Weed Out Mr. Wrong

We hope the "dream date" scenario with no second call is now easier for you to interpret. Now you can see that what may have been a great date in your eyes may not have been so great in his. If you liked him but played hard to get, he may think you don't like him. Now, he's too insecure to call. Or he may be a player who turned on the charm but never had any intention of calling again.

If you learn to read the signals men send, you can decipher their character and intentions early, before the second date, before you get too involved. Weed out the men who will give you only frustration and heartache. And don't let the "right guy" slip away by sending mixed or negative signals. Nurture the men who will give you the committed, sharing relationship you are looking for. Do this and you will be on the right course—with no unnecessary detours—to a relationship with good communication and minimal game playing.

Seven

THE DATING GAME: SUBSEQUENT DATES THROUGH COMMITMENT

If you have made it past the first date with that potential "Mr. Right," hold on, the ride only gets bumpier. Getting to know someone new can definitely be exhilarating, but negotiating the terrain of casual dating can also be confusing and difficult. This is the time when a relationship accelerates or comes to a standstill. This is also the time when women tend to get stuck in relationships going nowhere. The truth is, men often know right away when a relationship with a woman will never be more than casual, that he will never fall in love with her. At other times he may believe she has potential and so takes a "wait and see" attitude. How can a woman tell the difference?

In a guy's mind, the distinction between a woman who is "good for now" and a woman with "wife potential" is as clear as day. It is clear to him, but it may not be clear to you. He is certainly not going to break his neck making any effort to let you know in which category you fit. Since it is the rare man who will come out and say, "I like you, but I'll never love you," a woman, assuming she cares, needs to take the measure of his seriousness. What should women look out for?

How Serious Is He?

You can read how serious a man is about you by the *frequency and timing* of your dates together. If a guy wants to play it casual, he will always find an excuse to not go out with you on weekends, and he will not date you more than once a week, if that. Believe us, a man will conjure up the best excuses to keep his dates with a particular woman at a minimum. You may be dating a very busy professional man, but if he wanted to see you more often, he would. Date this guy if you like, but realize that it probably won't go very far. Get out and see other people because we can guarantee you that he is. If you enjoy being with him, follow his lead and keep him on your "wait till something better comes along" list. Use this as a chance to have fun and go out, but don't think of this guy as anything more than someone with whom to have fun.

We have all dated women who we knew were not Ms. Right. We liked them, had fun with them, and dated them once a week, tops. When they asked why we couldn't see them more often, we gave one excuse after another. We thought it was apparent that the relationship would never get very serious. Some women would fail to see the writing on the wall, allow themselves to get too attached, and wind up getting hurt.

If you are seeing him more than once a week, but nights out with him never include a weekend, he has not made up his mind as to just how interested in you he is. *Don't fall too hard too fast*. Weekend nights out are often very important play nights for professional men who work hard all week. If he is going out with the guys on the weekends, he is out there looking for someone else. But don't count this guy out yet, if you like him and are spending a lot of time together during the week. He is hesitant to commit but definitely enjoys your company. *If he is interested, he will soon start seeing you on the weekends. If he is not, he won't.*

If he does want to spend a weekend night out with you, that is a strong sign that he wants to develop the relationship further. Guys don't give up weekend nights for just anyone. If a guy has asked you out for a weekend night (and he hasn't called you at the last minute), then be aware that he is probably ready to take the relationship to the next level.

Are You Dating Very Frequently? Watch Out for Ulterior Motives

Of course, frequent dating isn't always what it seems. He may have ulterior motives. You may be getting asked out on date after date, including the weekends, and he may be paying a lot of attention to you. Beware. Men call this maneuver "the full court press," and it is designed to get a woman into bed as quickly as possible. His plan is to get you to feel as if the two of you have been dating for months when, in reality, you've only known each other for two weeks. If he continually tries to include alcohol in the plans and makes references to your spending the night, the deep relationship you may think you have formed is probably not headed where you think. If you convince yourself that the two of you have something special and have sex with this guy, you will see a rapid change once the act is consummated. He will be on to the next conquest and you will be left feeling bewildered and hurt. There is no need to be conned by this con artist once you know how to read his crystal-clear signals.

. . . Or He Is Inexperienced and This May Be a Flash in the Pan

There are other guys out there who will move things along rapidly and may not be out for sex but will find themselves losing interest just as quickly as they gained it. This is usually true of men who don't have much experience in dating women. A guy who hasn't been in many relationships may start dating you very frequently in the beginning because he enjoys your company and the idea of dating seems novel to him.

As soon as things get old and the novelty wears off, this guy may lose interest. He may suddenly wake up one day and realize he is in a relationship he doesn't want to be in. Unfortunately, there are no clear signals—besides obvious inexperience—that you could look for to avoid being hurt by a guy like this. There is little you can do. But that is no reason to beat yourself up or be hard on yourself because it didn't work out. *Consider it his loss.* This guy didn't have his mind clear.

Avoid Guys on the Rebound

Some guys will move things along very rapidly because they have just broken up with their ex-girlfriends. Once a comfortable relationship ends, they will often look to jump back into a similar situation as soon as possible. A woman is a security blanket. They like to continue having someone to call every day. They like to have sex on a regular basis. They don't know what it's like to be alone. Women who fall in love with men on the rebound are assured of getting hurt. He will get back together with his old girlfriend, or he will soon realize he needs time on his own. Either way, it spells p-a-i-n.

Here's a "sorry I got that guy on the rebound" story: A woman we know fell in love with a guy on the rebound. He was extremely attentive, attractive, intelligent, sincere—the kind of guy women love. One week after his girlfriend dumped him, our friend began dating him. A month later, she moved in. Every day they had sex, every day he told her he was crazy about her. They motor-biked, they Jet-Skied, they talked, they cooked. Eight months later, she was deeply in love with him. One day, while she was stirring the pasta, he told her he was getting back together with his old girlfriend. She would have to move out. She put down the wooden spoon and wept. It took her two years to get over it. Moral: Avoid men on the rebound; it is a no-win situation.

. . . And Men Who Have You on Their "Wait Till Something Better Comes Along" List

Have you ever been in a relationship where you spent a lot of time with a guy but there was no intensity? Perhaps you got check-in calls from him every week or so, maybe to make a date, maybe just to chat about nothing. You never talked about the relationship or your future together. You never spent any time together other than in the bedroom. Such situations never materialize into anything serious.

How many times did situations like this leave you confused and even hurt when this guy disappeared? He probably didn't want a relationship with you and was dating other women at the same time. All of the signals were there for you to know that this guy wasn't going to be around for long. He was talking to you often but the conversation was always lightweight. He just called you to check in, to make sure he was still in the picture. He wasn't asking you out with any regularity and the relationship wasn't progressing the way you wanted it to. However, you allowed yourself to rationalize the situation and stick it out, hoping he would come around. You settled and decided you would accept being treated worse than you would have liked. Ultimately, you wound up hurt by this guy and were left to wonder why.

When in Doubt, Ask Him

Take our advice. If things aren't progressing the way you would like them to and you aren't being treated the way you deserve, you need to take action. If you are certain he sees you as a girl who is only "good for now," stop seeing him. *He won't change his mind.* If you are unsure as to what your status is, talk to him and tell him how you feel. This is the best way to give a guy who is playing games with you a wake-up call. He will hear your demand to be treated well and will see that you will not stand for anything less. A man will respect your boldness and self-respect.

If he doesn't want to progress at a faster pace, then you'll have to walk. If he doesn't want to lose you, he will realize that you deserve to be treated better. A man will *never* let a woman with serious potential walk away. So, in the long run, you will be better off by talking to him.

What should you say? If you have been casually dating for a while, and you're not sure if he sees you as a "good for now" girl or as a woman with the potential to be his wife, there are ways to find out without making a scene. There is no need to be melodramatic. Simply say, "I like spending time with you. Do you want to spend more time together?" and watch his reaction. If he squirms or makes excuses, the relationship is going nowhere.

A girl Chris used to date took the initiative in this way. He liked her and they had a great time together, but he didn't see much of a future with her. They often went out to local bars, had a few drinks, played the jukebox, shot pool together. Often these nights would end up in the bedroom. Their relationship was casual and Chris was content with this, but she needed more. She told him how she felt. When Chris couldn't commit to seeing only her, she ended the relationship. She took a walk and found herself a boyfriend who gave her everything she needed. She avoided heartache, and is now happily engaged as a result of knowing what she wanted and acting on it.

Is He Mr. Wrong or Mr. Right?
Measure the Quality of His Attention

You can judge the seriousness of a man's intentions not only by the fact of his attention, but by its quality. A man with serious intentions will be earnest and will talk openly with you. He will call you at work and late at night. He wants to talk with you more often and about more interesting and relevant things. He will not just tell you stories about the last time he was drunk in Acapulco, he will tell you about his family. He may even mention that he would like you to meet them. The quality of his conversation should tell you that a more meaningful relationship is beginning to develop.

When we are serious about a woman, we make her a priority in our lives. Unlike the "good for now" girl we see when it is convenient, we make time for the woman we are interested in developing a serious relationship with. No matter how busy we are, we want to spend quality time with her. Often, this means we have to plan ahead rather than fitting her into our schedule at the last moment.

We prioritize her in other ways. When she has any kind of health problem, we call to find out how she is, what the doctor said, how we can help. We really care about her well-being, and we show that we care. In the same way, if she has an important job interview, or is waiting to hear from graduate schools, we are there with her, coaching her, concerned about her, cheering her on.

And here's another way to judge whether or not he sees you as someone with "serious potential": Is he losing interest in sex? Then you may be a "good for now" girl. After a while, we lose interest in having sex with someone we don't really like. Many women don't realize that men have feelings of sexual delicacy, but we do. Sooner or later, no matter how sexy a woman is and no matter how good the sex is at first, eventually, if we do not really care for her, the quality of the sex worsens.

Like women, we have feelings of sexual repulsion. When we are having sex with a women we don't have that much feeling for, eventually—it could be a week, a month, or six months—these feelings kick in. Our body urges us to copulate, but our mind says no. Eventually, we lose interest in having sex with her and try to avoid it. We pretend to be tired; we pretend to be asleep. When she seeks to arouse us, we squirm or play dead. When we are with a woman we really care about, we don't feel sexual repulsion. With her, quality sex remains quality sex.

By measuring the quality of his attention, you can measure his intentions toward you. When you know how to weed out the men who aren't serious about you, you will find yourself in more promising relationships.

Smooth the Path for Mr. Right:
Be Generous-Hearted

Once you recognize the potential for a long-term relationship, you will need to spend time together and see what develops. It seems to us that relationships, solid enough until this point, now proceed to break down for stupid reasons. Relationships collapse because men and women are so busy being defensive, playing games, and hiding their feelings that they have forgotten how important it is just to be nice to each other.

Compliment Him

If you care, show you care. Just as you like to be complimented, so do men. In fact, they require it. Tell him that he looks good or that he is a terrific guy. Compliment specific articles of clothing: "Great sneakers," "You look so handsome in that suit." Compliment his behavior: "You make me feel so good when I'm with you," "You're so attentive," "I have such a great time when we go out together." Tell him what a good impression he is making on your friends: "My best friend told me she thinks you're good for me. She also said she thinks you're really smart." Say anything positive about his job: "Your work sounds so interesting."

Guys are funny when it comes to compliments. If a man has taken a woman out to a restaurant and she comments on how delicious the food is, he will feel as if he, personally, caught that fish or killed that cow, seasoned and cooked it to perfection, and served it up for her delectation. If a man takes a woman out to see a movie and she really enjoys it and tells him so, he will feel as if he, personally, directed and produced that film. Your compliments make him feel confident and happy. They show him that you are sensitive to his needs and that you are making a conscious effort to make him feel good. *Once he knows this, he will feel more comfortable reciprocating and opening up to you.*

Everybody likes to be liked. Compliments won't go to his head and make him cocky. No matter how many people compliment him—his mother, his sister, his colleagues at work—there is nothing a man values more than being complimented by a woman he likes. A compliment coming from you will be different and will have a different effect than coming from anyone else.

Some men are so insecure that if you do not compliment them once in a while, they will begin to tell you that others have been telling them that they look good in an effort to get you to say it. Unfortunately, this usually backfires and causes women to get jealous. Such problems can be easily avoided by a simple compliment every so often. Don't hold back. Give him what he needs. Compliment him.

Buy Him Things

Women can be generous to men in deeds as well as words. Don't be afraid to bust open the piggy bank once in a while. A little can go a long way. Men love it when women offer to pay for something on a date or buy them some small thing as a token of their affection. This is an opportunity for a woman to step up to the plate and say, "I like you." By the second or third date, you can offer to pay for a round of drinks, or for the cab ride. It doesn't have to be something expensive; it is not the money but the gesture that counts. And we are shocked when women tell us they believe that they shouldn't have to pay for anything if they are having sex with a guy they are dating. Men don't like that mentality and what it suggests. Sex is no substitute for offering to pay for something once in a while.

When you buy something for a guy you are dating, you will be astonished by how touched he will be. This is especially true if it is not a gift-giving occasion. We are not talking about giving him a Rolex watch or Tiffany cuff links. A card or a CD will mean a lot to him.

We know that it may be tough to buy a man something he will actually like and use. Here are some rules of thumb so that you avoid blunders:

Do buy him something you think *he* will like, not just something *you* like. If your boyfriend likes Pearl Jam, buy him the new Pearl Jam CD. On the other hand, even though you may love roses, not many men we know enjoy receiving cut flowers.

Don't buy him something that is completely *not his style*. He will think you are trying to change him and he will resent you for it. Don't buy a man cologne if you have never known him to wear it. He won't use it, even if it's the greatest-smelling, most expensive cologne in the store.

Don't buy him bad clothing gifts, like a tie only his grandfather would wear, or khakis if he wears jeans, or Gucci shoes if he wears Timberland.

Don't buy him big practical things for his apartment like sheets, towels, or plates. These items are too domestic and personal for a woman to give a man. He may worry that you are thinking about moving in.

Do buy him small tchotchkes for his apartment: a scented candle, a picture, a clock.

Be wary about buying him a wallet or an organizer. Men are picky about such things. Unless you know his system and can duplicate it, don't try to buy him a system item. If it doesn't work in his system, your gift will just gather dust.

Do give him a framed picture of yourself, or of the two of you—if you are engaged.

Don't give him a framed picture of yourself, or of the two of you—if you have just started dating.

Cook for Him

We also hope you know that men have a soft spot for women who cook for them. Brad was dating a girl who enjoyed cooking and liked to cook for him. Not only was the food excellent, but her generosity hit its mark. He told his friends, and even his mother, what a great girl he had found. We know you know how important it is to score points with a man's mother. Brad's mother instantly liked this girl because she was taking care of her little boy. Once a man's mother likes a girl he is dating, the pressure put on him by his mother to stay with her intensifies. So buy your man a small gift or cook him dinner once in a while. It will show him how much you care, and it will strengthen the bond between you.

. . . Or Order in and Invite Him Over

If you can't cook or don't have the time, order in and invite him over. It goes just as far, as Rich can attest. His girlfriend is often too busy to cook but did want to do something to show her appreciation of him. Instead of putting the effort into cooking, she put the effort into setting the scene. She put some soft, romantic music on, lit a few candles, and dimmed the lights. She set the table, poured some wine, and wore her best dress. When the cartons of Chinese food and fortune cookies arrived, all she had to do was serve the food. Rich appreciated her efforts immensely and her generosity fueled his own.

Generosity Works

Any man who feels that you care about him will like you more. Throughout Rich and Marla's relationship, Marla showed incredible understanding about his hectic work schedule and never resorted to playing games with him. When they met, Rich was a first-year resident and had many nights on call at the hospital, but Marla made it easy for him to develop a relationship with her even at this busy time in his career. She understood his situation and appreciated any opportunity she had to spend with him.

She didn't end her social life with her friends either. When Rich was busy working, she didn't complain that he never had time for her. She made it very easy for Rich to realize that she truly cared for him and was willing to be patient to give their relationship a chance to evolve. Most girls Rich had dated previously were not able to work around his busy schedule. Marla's understanding and support made her stand out from all the others. As a result of her actions, Rich thought of her as the most generous, caring, sweet, and independent woman he had ever met. He soon fell in love and committed himself to her.

Women seem to worry that if they put too many cards on the table and show their hands, men will lose interest in them. So they resort to manipulative tactics like playing hard to get. Remember, men hate these kinds of mind games. Don't toy with his feelings and spoil a good thing. If you meet a man halfway and do the little things that count so much, he will be more willing to open up to you. He will trust you and feel comfortable with you. Save time and strengthen the bond between you, don't waste time and get involved in game playing or saving face.

Getting Serious

As the two of you get more serious, you will be seeing each other more often and in situations other than "dates." You will be doing chores together. You can help him shop for clothes or for some furniture for his apartment. He will help you drag your new stereo system home. A man will realize that his feelings for you are growing stronger. You are becoming much more important to him. With these feelings come a lot of drastic changes in his lifestyle. He knows that he wants to spend more and more time with you, which means less and less time with his friends and other women.

His free time will now be spent with you. All of a sudden he has a "girlfriend," and you are a friend and a companion, someone who means much more to him than anyone he has dated casually. Most important, he now realizes that he is vulnerable. He is susceptible to pain and heartache. His powerful emotions for you have made him feel a bit out of control. Men hate this.

Nevertheless, he will usually be straight with himself. He knows that you now hold incredible power over him. He realizes that if you leave him, he will be devastated. He may try to fend off these feelings and resist getting closer because he fears vulnerability. It is his nature to try to remain free and uncommitted for as long as possible despite what he is truly feeling inside.

Bringing Up the "C" Word

Why are men so terrified of falling in love and committing to one woman? Why does the very thought petrify us? To a man, commitment means a loss of privacy, a loss of freedom. It means that he has to stop chasing and dating other women. Commitment also means vulnerability. He can be hurt now.

One of our Maker's little tricks on us was to make women love commitment and like talking about it. Men are made of different stuff. We need commitment, but fear it. If we had our way, we would *never* talk about commitment. Relationships pass through different levels of commitment, but whether it is committing to monogamy or to marriage, we still hate to pin ourselves down in words.

Women are the ones who need to bring up the topic of the relationship and where it is going because a man won't.

He sees this as a woman's job. And when you do bring it up, even when he wants to be with you, even when he doesn't want to date anyone else, he'll think, Uh-oh. He will be uncomfortable. He will feel his freedom slipping away. He knows he's committed to you, but he doesn't want to admit it. He knows you can hold his words against him at a later date.

There is a right and a wrong time to bring up commitment. Women who bring up the topic obscenely early in a relationship give womanhood a bad name. Brad had been dating one woman for about two months when she dragged him over to the engagement-ring counter at Tiffany's. She was thinking marriage; meanwhile, he hadn't even committed to an exclusive relationship yet! We suggest you not force things so soon. Men get completely turned off. They think you want marriage or commitment, not him. When women put the pressure on too soon, men close down or run away. So, if things are going well, relax and allow the relationship to develop naturally.

Some relationships evolve slowly, while others seem to develop more quickly. A number of things in a relationship become implied over time, for example, seeing each other on weekend nights, spending time with each other's families, and not dating other people. As the relationship deepens, you will start taking vacations together, going on weekend getaways, and including each other in future plans. If you are seeing your boyfriend on a regular basis, especially on weekends, and are sleeping over at each other's apartments and having good sex, the chances are that he knows as well as you do that he is in a committed relationship.

We admit that there comes a time when you must do a reality check and evaluate the relationship you are in. Is it going somewhere? Or is he just another guy who, like all the rest, will soon become a distant memory? You have every right to know where you stand in a relationship. All we advocate is that you try to be patient and allow him the time and space he needs to commit to you and only you.

If it is important to you to move your relationship to the commitment level, you will need to bring it up in the right way. Try to do this without making him feel pressured and overwhelming him. We suggest you introduce the topic at a time when he is at ease and comfortable. This might be at the end of an evening when you had dinner together, maybe saw a movie, and had good sex. As you lie there talking about everything from "If you were a tree, what kind of tree would you be?" to the state of the nation, you might say something about the goodness of the moment and how close you have become. This can be the spark he needs to tell him that the relationship is progressing to the next level. It will make him understand that he needs to talk with you about where you stand with each other.

He may avoid the topic right then in order to buy himself time to think things through, but he will know he has an obligation to you to address the subject sooner rather than later. Allow us to emphasize that you will need to handle this situation with kid gloves. There is a fine line between planting a seed in his mind and scaring him with too much pressure. Resist giving him an ultimatum. This might just spur a defensive, hostile reaction. Instead, just gently describe your own deepening feelings.

After Rich and Marla were dating for a while, the topic of commitment was on both of their minds. Rich knew he loved Marla, but he, like most men, was afraid of commitment. He was even more afraid of verbally expressing his feelings and telling Marla that he wanted to be with only her. He didn't know what to do or how to express his deep emotions. As a result, he said nothing and hoped that his actions would speak for themselves.

Marla, on the other hand, wanted and needed to hear Rich verbally commit to her. She waited longer than she wanted to wait, but finally brought up the topic. She gave him the classic ultimatum: "I don't want you seeing other women, and if you won't commit to me, I don't want to see you again." Rich's reaction to Marla's ultimatum was shock and anger. He was shocked that this sweet woman he had fallen in love with was being so confrontational. He then became angry because it seemed as if she was forcing him to say, "I don't want to be with any other woman but you," although he did feel that way and indeed was not seeing anyone else. He felt as if he were being attacked and pushed into a corner. In a foolish, defensive reaction fueled by his male pride, he abruptly said, "I'm not ready to commit to you." It was an ugly conversation that should not have ended as it did.

After ten days of not talking to each other, Rich and Marla spoke again. This time they had a more gentle, open, and honest conversation. Marla told Rich that she truly enjoyed spending time with him, felt as if she were growing closer to him, and hoped that they could be together in the future. Rich felt the same way and told her so. It was the first time they openly discussed their feelings for each other and it was a defining moment in their relationship. Rich felt more at ease in talking about his deep feelings when he was not being challenged or forced to say anything. This time Marla made it easy for him to open himself up and speak from his heart. The conversation ended with Marla knowing that Rich loved her and that he would be there for her in the future.

The key to getting a man to make a verbal commitment—

whether to monogamy or to marriage—is to avoid pressuring him or forcing him to say or do anything. Instead, just describe how you feel. Express that you are not interested in seeing other men. And ask him if he feels the same way. Men are not stupid; we know where our duty lies. We just hate feeling pressured or forced to make important decisions before we are ready. So give us time.

After six months of seriously dating a woman, a man will feel some level of commitment to her. So, if you have been dating him for six months or longer, and you need him to verbally commit to you, tell him how you feel.

If you have repeatedly tried to get him to commit verbally to not seeing other women and working toward a future together, and he won't, it is time for you to move on.

Your Goal: Be Wary of Getting Stuck in Relationships Going Nowhere, Be Generous in Relationships Going Somewhere

You should find men who have no intention of getting serious with you fairly easy to spot. After you've measured the quantity and quality of his attention and realize he's not interested, you may—with grace and confidence—weed these guys out of your life. It is the men who are ambivalent, those who are stalled in a "wait and see attitude," who are more difficult to read. You worry that he may be taking advantage of you; you worry that if you press him too hard to commit, he will bail out.

If you know he is the right guy for you, and you are certain he cares, give him the space and time to get used to the idea, to build up his courage and the confidence that you are the woman for him. Men are usually slower than women in coming to this realization. If you are generous and trusting, this will make it easier for him to trust and be comfortable with you. Don't give out any ultimatums. Opening up a discussion about how you feel about each other will wake him up to his duty to discuss his intentions with you sooner rather than later.

Eight

~~~~~~

SEX

Men don't usually tell women the nitty-gritty of men's sexual desire, probably because they don't want to scare women away—or incite a riot.

If men do speak their minds in mixed company, they pretty things up, they omit certain ugly facts. Well, we think women need to hear the truth about men and sex. So, hold on to your hats (and your tempers); what we will say about sex may not be pretty, it may not even be reasonable, but it is what men think.

We'll start by answering the most popular question women ask us about sex: Is it okay for a woman to have sex with a man on the first date? Men will want to break our necks for telling it like it is and hurting their chances, but allow us to level with you. The answer is no. Assuming a woman is interested in more than sex, which she usually is, then having sex on the first date is a bad idea.

When It Comes to Sex,
Men Still Believe in the Double Standard

A man still holds a woman to a stricter sexual standard than he holds himself to. No man wants to think of his girlfriend or future wife as promiscuous. We know this sounds old-fashioned, but it is true. When a man chooses a woman, he would like all her prior sexual experiences to be deleted, so to speak. Or, at the very least, eclipsed. It makes the hair on the back of any man's neck stand up when he thinks of his woman sleeping with another man. So, if a woman sleeps with a man on the first date, no matter what she says, a man will think she's promiscuous.

The first question that will enter his mind is whether she does this with everyone. And do you know what? Women are kind enough to answer that question for us without our even asking them. After the act is completed, a woman will inevitably say, "I just want you to know that I don't do this all the time." Sorry, ladies, if you didn't know it before, know it now—no man believes this line. Some men chuckle to themselves when they hear it. Some guys may even count the seconds after the act is completed, timing how long it takes for her to voice the inevitable disclaimer.

The same rules apply for oral sex. A man finds it hard to believe that a woman he hardly knows could put his penis in her mouth. When a woman performs oral sex on a first date—or even the very night we meet her—we say to ourselves, I can't believe I just met this woman and now she has my penis in her mouth. We find this amazing. A woman doesn't know what rock we climbed out from under, but, nevertheless, our penis is in her mouth. Consider how much greater our amazement will be when a woman agrees to engage in sexual intercourse on the first date.

During a couple's first few encounters, he is still sizing her up. If you have sex too soon, he will wonder to himself, How many guys were here before me? He will believe that you do not require emotional ties to get sexual satisfaction. So, he won't feel compelled to provide them, then or ever.

The truth is that underneath all our sexual bravado, men are more conservative and more idealistic than women. At least we are when it comes to choosing a wife. An unattached man will take what he can get sexually, but he will always have his eye out for that special woman he can respect and trust. He will give up his freedom for nothing less. In practical terms, this means that if a woman is interested in love and marriage—as opposed to just fun—there is really no good reason to have sex early in the relationship. This may or may not sit well with women, but this is what men think.

There's No Such Thing as the Special Chemistry "Exception"

How about those magical times when you meet a man and feel the shock of that special chemical reaction? Why not follow your instincts?

Imagine the scenario: You meet him, a stranger, maybe at a club or a party, and end up talking for an hour or two. You give him your telephone number and pray that he calls you. Meanwhile, you ask your friends and associates if they know him. You find out that a colleague of yours has a best friend who knows of him through the social scene. This best friend of your colleague tells you that he is the nicest guy a woman could ever meet. He is sweet, caring, successful, and funny.

A day later he calls you and asks you to dinner. The two of you have so much in common, before you know it you have been talking on the phone with the guy for an hour. Finally, you both agree that it is getting late and it would be best for the two of you to get to bed. The man asks you to see him the very next night instead of Friday night as originally planned. You say that it would be your pleasure. As you hang up the phone, you want to call your best friend to tell her about what a perfect guy this man seems. You then realize she is fast asleep and would not appreciate such a call. Finally, you slip under your cozy comforter and doze off, awakening the next morning in an optimistic mood despite your lack of sleep.

The next evening the man picks you up to take you to a great restaurant where you eat a delicious dinner, sip white wine, and talk heart-to-heart. At your door, the good-night kiss is better than you imagined. You ask him in for a few minutes, since it is chilly outside. The next thing you know you find yourself on your bed, the two of you completely naked and engaging in hot, passionate sex. After falling asleep for a couple of hours, he decides to leave so he doesn't oversleep for an important meeting in the morning. The next day at work you wonder whether you went too far this time. You think to yourself, He is definitely the man for me. He must know I don't have sex so soon with every guy. I just hope he trusts me as I trust him.

Men are not as trusting as women. This man may not call you again. If the date had ended at your door, there would be little doubt that he would call you—now there is doubt. Most men will feel discomfort or a slackening of interest after bedding a woman so fast and so easily. He may find you an incredible turn-on, he may be crazy about you, but he will be less likely to become serious about you.

He May Be Testing You

Men use sex to test a woman's character. If he isn't interested in getting seriously involved with a promiscuous woman, then he might see how far she is willing to go with him sexually and judge her by it. A case in point: Brad was out at his beach house one summer. He met a beautiful woman who he felt had some very special qualities. He knew her through some friends, but had never been out with her alone. On their first night out, they went to a popular club and drank and danced all night. They partied until 4:00 A.M. and then went back to the house. They found a room that was unoccupied and attacked each other like hungry animals that hadn't eaten in weeks. Everything happened that early morning. It was very satisfying, sexually speaking, for Brad. He definitely wanted another night with this woman. But he did not want a relationship with her. She was now classified as a fun, party girl, not a girl to have a relationship with and bring home to Mom.

A Man May Delay Having Sex with a Woman If He Really Likes Her

A man who likes a woman may not even try to have sex with her on the first few dates. By not initiating sex, or by gently keeping her within limits, the man keeps alive the belief that he didn't and couldn't sleep with her early in the relationship. This is to avoid any mental confusion later on when he feels that he has to make a decision as to whether she is the right woman for him. Chris once found himself in this situation with a woman he really liked. She was his dream come true. At least it seemed that way in such a short period of time. By the third date, they were very comfortable together. The night went from dinner to drinks to a late-night coffee. They just didn't want the date to end. They proceeded to Chris's apartment to listen to his extensive music collection. Next thing they knew, they found themselves rolling around in Chris's bed. Things were proceeding smoothly, maybe too smoothly. But when Chris realized that the next act would be intercourse, he began to slow things down. She kept pulling Chris on top of her as an indication of what she expected next. But Chris really liked her and felt he might have some kind of future with her. He didn't want to jeopardize the potential relationship. He wanted to get to know her before having sex with her, even if she didn't care either way. Essentially, he was preserving her potential.

Unfortunately, she was bewildered. She felt she didn't turn him on enough for him to complete the act. You are probably thinking that Chris should have explained the situation to her to ease her insecurity. Actually, he couldn't, because he was afraid she would tell him that she was willing to go further. A man in this situation prefers not to know how far he *could* have gone. He prefers to leave that a mystery. Any discussion might reveal the woman's willingness to go all the way. In the end, Chris preserved her "good girl" status and this made him feel better about her, but it may have been achieved at her expense emotionally.

For both man and woman, this situation is very delicate. Women expect relentless sexual pursuit, so when we act like gentlemen and not like animals, they are bewildered. Please help us on this one. Don't be confused and hurt if we don't make the move to consummate the relationship in the first few dates. You know very well when the man you are with is turned on by you. You can see for yourself when he is dying to have sex, but groping for self-restraint. Don't torment us by expecting us to play Casanova when you really want us to be Prince Charming, the Mr. Right you have been dreaming about.

Either There Is Sexual Chemistry or There Isn't

The truth is, a woman shouldn't worry about whether or not a man is attracted enough, because he either is or isn't. Unlike women, men feel sexual attraction right away or never. A woman finds this confusing, especially if she is with a man and they get along really well and have a great time together. Why aren't they having sex? She should be able to read his signals. If he is clearly attracted, then she shouldn't worry. He may be delaying out of shyness or because he really likes her and wants to preserve the relationship's potential. Sexual chemistry is not something that a man can manufacture, even though he may try if he's drunk and she's willing.

If, after a few dates, he has made no moves on you, you might be in a friendship, not a love affair. Brad once dated a woman he loved to spend time with. He went out with her four nights a week because he genuinely enjoyed her company. They didn't always have elaborate plans. Sometimes they just hung out at each other's apartment talking about everything. When it came time for something sexual to occur, Brad tried to back out in any way possible. He always asked himself why. He always asked Rich and Chris why. It was very confusing to him at the time, and most probably to this woman as well. Brad wanted to be sexually attracted to her, but just couldn't force himself to be. A man might manufacture every excuse in the book for you in the hope that he will "snap out of it." But a man cannot "snap out" of something like this. A man's attraction for a woman is a physical reality. It either is there or it isn't.

If there is that chemical reaction, when *is* the right time to start having sex? When there is intimacy and trust, of course. You be the judge of when. *As a rule of thumb, we would recommend that you have sexual intercourse no sooner than the fifth date*. Anything sooner will be too soon. A guy will not know you well enough before then. His tendency will be to stop concentrating on the woman and the relationship and to start focusing on the sex. He'll start seeing you to get laid.

This shouldn't mean that there isn't any sexual contact before the fifth date. We just don't recommend having intercourse with him until you've dated him at least five times.

And once you are in a stable relationship, then you can throw caution to the winds and express your desire. When you're in a relationship with a future, you can be demure if you feel like it, or you can be outrageous and wild. The point is, he knows you now and will not make snap judgments.

What Do Men Want Sexually?

So, what do men really want sexually? *Most of all, a man wants a woman with sexual power*. By this we mean that she attracts him. She is his type. There is a chemical reaction. This is the woman who makes his heart start pumping overtime as soon as she enters the room. But more than this, for men, a woman with real sexual power—power with a lifelong hold on a man—is a woman with a sense of her own worth, a woman with confidence, with spirit, at home with herself and happy in her own body. We're not only talking about physical prettiness. If you have ever talked to a stripper or a model, you'll know that the most physically pretty women are often the most insecure. Such a woman may have a fleeting sexual power over a man, but it is not the kind of power that lasts.

A woman with sexual power is not ashamed of her body; she is proud of it. After sex, she is not afraid to walk across the room naked. She conveys confidence in the way she moves, in the way she kisses, in the way she knows how to please and be pleased. She is not afraid to tell him what she likes. She is willing to do what he wants to do, and knows how to accentuate the experience. A woman with sexual power allows a man to take the lead and knows how to follow. She knows when it is her turn to lead. She is able to command the mutuality of the sexual experience.

For a Man, Sexual Compatibility Can Make or Break the Relationship

We know that sex is as important to women as it is to us, but women have told us that their priorities are different from ours. A woman may choose a man who is not absolutely the lover of her dreams because he happens to be extremely bright, or very good-hearted, or terribly rich. A man is less able to make such adjustments. We must emphasize how important, indeed crucial, sex is for a man. The chemistry has to be there, especially in the beginning, and despite the fluctuating hills and valleys that will inevitably occur in all long-term relationships. Bad or lukewarm sex, especially in a new relationship, spells incompatibility. Good sex gone bad may mean the relationship is on the skids.

His Sense of Himself As a Man Is Tied in to His Sexual Performance

Not only is good sex crucial to a man, his very sense of himself as a man is tied in to his sexual performance—and your satisfaction. Manhood is all about performance. When his manhood is at stake, you can be sure he's not going to take many risks. Since performing well is so important to men, they will opt out of sex rather than risk not performing well. A man in an established relationship may not want to have sex simply because he is not in the mood. He may be tired, or watching sports, or he may even have a problem at work on his mind.

Remember, sex is physically demanding, and it is usually the man who does most of the "work." He must become erect, stay erect, perform the act, not ejaculate too quickly but make sure he ejaculates eventually. There is much more, but these are the broad strokes (no pun intended). He also needs to provide the woman with the emotion she needs and deserves. This makes the situation even more of an undertaking. And that's after a full day's work in the operating room, the courtroom, or the boardroom. Sometimes a man thinks it's better to avoid having sex if he is not ready to give her a full 100 percent effort.

So, you should not take it personally if your man doesn't always want to have sex on demand. Sex requires energy. A man has to be ready for the challenge, and this is not always the case. It doesn't mean that he is not attracted to you or doesn't love you anymore. It doesn't mean that he has found another woman or is thinking about ending the relationship. Men, any more than women, just aren't physically and emotionally "available" all the time. Men would love you to know this because it is a knock on our manhood when you are persistent about having intercourse and we don't want to. Even a bigger knock on our manhood is when we cannot perform up to par when we are expected to.

What Men Want Sexually: The Details

Let us tell you truthfully what is important to a man sexually. Every man has a favorite position. And it is important to a man that his partner is pleased and pleases him in this favored position. For him, that spells compatibility. If a woman objects, there is no way the man will be satisfied. It is like telling a pizza lover he will never again be able to eat pizza if he marries you. If the man is in love, he will try to adjust. But sexual preferences are hard to change; somehow, it's in the blood.

Men also experiment with different positions and like women who are open to trying new things. During sex, many men will vary positions while relying on the "old reliable" position as the "bread and butter." A woman who is rigid in this way may very well turn a man off. Sex should not be a wrestling match. One such wrestling match occurred between Chris and a woman he met at his health club. They were having sex in the missionary position when Chris attempted to change the position, but she resisted his move. She did not say anything to Chris, so he was left feeling bewildered. To make matters worse, he didn't feel comfortable in talking with her about it right there and then, so he had to rely on nonverbal communication. In the end, that sexual encounter seemed wearisome to him.

Sometimes, when a man and a woman just don't know each other well enough, sex can be awkward. Good sex happens when there is a spirit of openness. When a couple knows how to communicate—physically and verbally—they are able to work out the small kinks together. They can guide each other to a mutually satisfying sexual experience.

Orgasm: Hers

Giving sexual pleasure to a woman is, for a man, one of life's greatest satisfactions. We understand that there might be some women who do not necessarily need an orgasm in order to have a fulfilling sexual experience, but men are still genuinely concerned that their partner reaches orgasm. This is especially true if they are in love. As a matter of fact, if a woman cannot have an orgasm with her boyfriend for an extended period of time, the relationship will suffer a strain. The man will begin to try harder and harder, and so will his girlfriend. This is the formula for disaster. The woman may even resort to faking an orgasm to alleviate the pressure. It may seem like a good idea at the time, but if a man finds out, believe us, damage will be done.

Men understand that it may not be easy for a woman to have an orgasm. If the sexual relationship between a man and a woman is a healthy one, and both parties are often satisfied, a woman can let a man know that it's not going to happen this time. Neither man nor woman can achieve an orgasm on any given date, time, or location. She should just make it clear in a nice, caring way that she will not be able to reach a climax but that she is still enjoying the experience. Even though a man does have a fragile ego, he understands the subtlety of a woman's sexual response and will not be too badly hurt by her revelation. If a woman begins faking orgasms, giving her partner the false sense that he can have her reach orgasm each and every time, she is venturing into dangerous territory. When a man concludes that she is a faker, he will never trust that he is ever doing the right thing and, as a result, the relationship will suffer.

Men need help in knowing how to satisfy a particular woman. Every woman is so different. We find it hard to understand why women are so silent when we know one thing must feel better than another. Sometimes it appears that a woman feels so uncomfortable saying what she likes that she would rather forgo her own pleasure than tell a man what to do. Why not tell us? We won't be offended by some instruction. It's your body, and it's your enjoyment. Make the most of it. It's a turn-on for men to hear a woman tell us what she likes while we are doing it. Then we know to continue to do what we are doing.

Do men really know whether or not a woman had an orgasm? Many times the answer is no. How do we know if you do not tell us? Some women find it hard to believe that a man cannot tell. But many times we just can't. If you are in a long-term relationship with a man, and he knows the nuances of your body and your reactions, he might be able to read you. In all other situations, a man is in the dark. Remember, every woman is unique. The point is, please let us know that we did the trick. We feel foolish when we are still striving for it and it already happened. We presume that it puts you on the spot as well. Not wanting to upset the man, you probably feel uncomfortable having to answer the question "Did you come?" when it was an unsuccessful attempt. Talk to us, please.

Talking Dirty

In general, men love vocal women who enjoy having sex. We don't know a man in the world who is not excited when he hears a woman tell him she likes what he is doing. "You feel so good inside me," "Harder, baby, harder." Yes, even well-brought-up girls of sterling character may "talk dirty" in bed. It is erotic, and men love it. Things that are taboo under normal circumstances are okay in bed. We are not saying you should become a complete animal if that is not you. We are just saying that some playful talking can be fun. A man may look at a woman who is too shy in bed as a boring sexual partner. There is no need to be bored or boring when a small amount of "dirty talk" requires little effort. Test his excitability with one or two phrases. Every man loves at least a little bit of this while the two of you are rolling around.

Alternatively, men dislike women who act as if they were trying to win an Academy Award. Such women take things too far. It is hard to explain this because there is no clear-cut line, but women know when they are acting and when they aren't. Overacting should be left for B movies and porn flicks, not real life. A good example of this is when Brad was having sex with a somewhat older woman at her apartment one winter night. She was screaming his name, talking dirty, grinding, moaning, using her fingernails on his back, grabbing the bedcovers, and engaging in just about all the other possible options available to a woman who is having intercourse. It was exciting for him at first, but he soon began to laugh to himself at her obvious attempt to be a porn star. What started as a turn-on ended up being a turnoff. She went too far. The moral of the story is, try and be yourself; for the right man that will be enough.

Men love it when women are genuinely enthusiastic about sex. And "talking dirty" shows your enthusiasm and excites a man's imagination.

Oral Sex: Hers

What does turn a man on is performing oral sex on a woman, especially a woman he loves. This is a very intimate act for a man, and it will boost his ego if the woman enjoys it. However, if a woman is not well-groomed, or doesn't smell nice, a man may not perform oral sex. If a woman enjoys receiving oral sex and wishes a man to do it more often, she should tell him but she should also be sensitive to his concerns. Did we say that in a politically correct manner? We hope so. Also, because the act is so intimate, a man may not perform oral sex on a woman when he feels he can be selfish, or when he really isn't very interested in her. We personally believe that sex is the place for giving and receiving. Where there is trust, there should be pleasure. Why not be generous?

Oral Sex: His

As every woman surely knows, every man is greatly turned on by having her perform oral sex on him. And a man likes to watch a woman while she does this. Not only is the physical sensation unspeakably pleasurable, watching a woman perform oral sex on him boosts a man's ego. Men get turned on by being in control. On the other hand, women tell us they feel powerful turning a man on in this way, so, hopefully, in the act of fellatio there is satisfaction all around.

Another reason a man likes to receive oral sex from his partner is the "bad girl" image the man has in his mind. Although we say we love a woman of sterling character, we desire a "wild" girl in bed too. Moreover, a man will *continually* think back to the woman or women in his past who

allowed him to ejaculate in her mouth. Why is this so pleasurable for a man? It is because there is no interruption or
change in the stimulation, which could take away from the
enjoyment. Men greatly appreciate a woman who will do
this for them. We don't care whether or not you swallow it.
We know that it cannot possibly taste good.

We repeat, men do love fellatio and might reconsider
remaining in a relationship with a woman who refuses. A
man cannot understand why a woman who purports to love
him so much will not do something for him he enjoys so
tremendously. This is one of the few times in a man's life
when he can relax and receive pleasure. If the woman has a
problem performing oral sex, this needs to be discussed,
especially if there seem to be problems in the relationship
regarding sex. This could be the reason for his losing interest in her sexually.

Fellatio: What Men Want

Our female friends wanted to know what pleases men most
during oral sex. They wanted to hear the fine points. And
they were embarrassed to ask their boyfriends. "What's the
most important thing to do?" they wanted to know. So we
told them. To maximize a man's pleasure, the most important thing to do is to maintain a continuous up-and-down
rhythmic motion with the mouth and hand. "What does
that mean?" they asked.

We supplied the details. Her mouth should cover the head
of his penis, with her hand directly beneath, gripping him
firmly. Move the hand and mouth up and down in unison.
The mouth should move as far down the shaft as possible.
On the upstroke her hand should go up to the base of the
head. Start slowly and build to a faster pace.

"How fast?" they asked. Not too fast or his penis will lose sensation. Just keep a constant, moderate pace. It also increases his pleasure if she uses tongue motions while his penis is in her mouth.

"Even though stopping causes a momentary break in the rhythm, isn't it pleasurable for him to have his penis lightly licked or caressed?" our friends wanted to know. This will certainly excite him at the beginning of oral sex, but after continuous stroking, a man really can't feel that delicate sensation. When our friends then told us women sometimes did this to rest the jaw, we made a suggestion. One thing a woman can do while taking a break is to continue stroking his penis with her hand. She will also drive him wild if, at the same time, she licks or caresses the base of the scrotum, a very sensitive part of the male anatomy.

"What shouldn't a woman do when giving oral sex to a man?" our women friends asked. Don't use teeth. Don't lean an elbow on his thigh—it hurts. Don't break the rhythm by delicately licking the penis and stopping the continuous stroke. Don't stop until he's finished.

Being Private in Public

Men like to have sex in different places. How are we to know where your man likes to have sex the most? We can tell you that variety is the spice of life and that men think it is fun to experiment with new and exciting places. Men often like to try out public places for their sexual adventures. The possibility of being caught in a forbidden act adds spice. One night a friend of ours was in a trendy bar in downtown Manhattan when he ran into a young woman he had dated months before. They had both had quite a bit to drink that evening and were soon making out as if they were the only ones in the bar. The woman grabbed him by the hand, and they descended down the steps on their way to the women's bathroom. They both entered the stall having not said a single word to each other. The rest will be left to your fertile imagination.

Another example of this occurred when Chris and his girlfriend were out on a date on the Upper East Side of Manhattan one night. This was a time when Chris lived in the suburbs north of New York City. After meeting, they both decided to go to Chris's apartment by cab. The cab ride was a long one, so they decided to start the fireworks a little early. Let's put it this way: The cabdriver didn't charge them a nickel for the forty-five-minute trip.

Okay, so that may be too much for you to handle, or you've already done that and more. There are some things you can do that are just as exciting as the scenarios discussed above yet are not as risky, such as sex in your own car in the country. Boy, will your boyfriend look forward to those long drives upstate to see the leaves turn in the fall. Or sex in movie theaters. Why not let your boyfriend lift your skirt and touch you during those love scenes in *9½ Weeks*? Or why don't you touch him? Don't be shy. Sometimes it's fun to be a little naughty.

The Importance of Underwear

Men also love sexy lingerie. Some women understand this, others don't. Wearing beautiful underclothes shows that you have a sexy quality that you yourself recognize and enjoy. You exude a certain confidence that, in turn, excites men. If you are wearing something strange that looks terrible, we think that you don't know how to be sexy. Men ask the next question very often: Why does she wear that big, grandma-style underwear? To men, a woman is supposed to have a sexy quality. Wearing sexy lingerie accomplishes this. We do understand that women, like men, want to be comfortable. Can you be comfortable and sexy too? Please work with us on this one. Don't wear underwear your grandmother would wear. Get to the store and get some fabulous underclothes and sleepwear. Believe us, it's an investment that will pay special dividends.

Masturbation as Necessity

Have you ever asked yourself why men need to masturbate? Did it ever disturb you that your boyfriend would masturbate even though he had you? Did you ever feel insecure because he was masturbating, thinking that he was losing interest in you? We will tell you what masturbation means to a man. Hopefully, this will ease your fears and suspicions. Just for starters, a man involved in the healthiest, most exciting, and fulfilling relationship still needs to masturbate. Don't fool yourself either. If you have a boyfriend, yes, he is masturbating despite what you might think. The line that a woman in denial always gives is, "Not my boyfriend, he doesn't need to masturbate, he has me to take care of all his sexual urges." Ladies, wake up and smell the coffee; your man is pleasuring himself when you don't know it.

First of all, masturbating fulfills his need for sexual variety. By nature, men crave more than one partner. When masturbating, a man can think about whatever or whomever he chooses, which helps to satisfy his need for sexual variety. Guys like to think of other women. This does not mean that a man wants this type of sex or this type of woman in his life, it just tickles his fancy. In no way do men think about this as cheating, and in no way should women feel that it is.

If you feel left out, why not play a part in his masturbation? That doesn't mean that your hand has to take over. While he masturbates, you can help enhance his pleasure by caressing him. He can then caress you while you masturbate. Simultaneous masturbation is also a nice variation on intercourse. Nobody can please you like you can please yourself, so why not do it together? This will certainly turn your partner on. A man loves to watch his lover touch herself. It is very erotic and enticing to a man. There are plenty of men who enjoy having a woman watch while they are masturbating as well. There is nothing wrong with this. It adds a nice wrinkle to a couple's sex life. You cannot be shy, though. It can be difficult getting used to someone watching because it is usually a very private act. Once you feel comfortable, it can be very enjoyable.

A man will also use masturbation as a way to relieve tension and as an aid in falling asleep. After a man has an orgasm, he feels more relaxed than if he had gotten a massage. Perhaps you have watched your lover falling into a deep doze only minutes after sex. Some men, who sleep alone, will masturbate every night in order to fall asleep more easily. This may sound a bit strange, but it is true. The act requires very little in the way of emotion, exertion, or conversation. Even men who live with their girlfriends or are married masturbate. It satisfies many needs for the man without requiring much effort.

Post-Coital Realities: Fatigue or Flight

This brings us to the delicate subject of sexual fatigue. Women shouldn't take it personally when a man falls asleep immediately after he climaxes. Women must come to grips with the fact that a man becomes extremely tired after he has an orgasm. This feeling is like trying to stay awake after you have taken sleeping pills. To try and fight the feeling is nearly impossible. Not only is the man very tired, but he has an incredible feeling of relaxation. All his muscles go into a relaxed state. A man will then become very mellow and will only want to lie there like a bag of potatoes.

So you ask, if a man is so relaxed and tired after an orgasm, why does he get up and run out the door like a track star after we've finished having sex? A man also loses all his sexual desire after he reaches his climax. Although there are exceptions to this rule, *it is true for the majority of men out there*. Let's consider this situation: A man is all worked up and having sex with a woman for whom he has little or no feelings. It seems as if he is very turned on. As soon as it is over, his personality changes. Since the man's sexual desire is sated, then the sexual feelings he had for that women are down the drain as well. If there are no emotional feelings, then there is nothing left. A man looks at her and wonders what he is doing there. It is similar to waking up from a dream. You wonder what the hell happened. One second you are doing and saying things that you normally wouldn't, and then you have this overwhelming feeling that you have to leave.

It's funny what an orgasm can do to a man. After a climax, the overwhelming feeling of exhaustion may be countered by the overwhelming feeling of needing to leave. Which one wins? Well, a man will determine how badly he needs to leave. If it is bad enough, there is no level of exhaustion that will keep him there. To be blunt, a man has a feeling of disgust after climaxing when he discovers that he is with a woman he doesn't really like. This does not necessarily mean that the two will never sleep together again. The sexual feelings do come back eventually. Sometimes it takes weeks, days, hours, or minutes, but most of the time the feelings do return. If they don't, this man will not call again. What happened? At some point, the man remembers the feeling he had after sex and realizes that it isn't worth it to go back to that woman. Repulsion outweighs sexual desire. Sometimes this happens after one encounter with a woman and sometimes it happens after dozens of encounters with that woman. At some point, the sexual feelings run out when they are not bolstered by emotional attachment. And then the man will end the affair. Do you see why we suggest women be sexually cautious at the beginning of a relationship?

It is generally a good sign when a man stays the night. But, really, all you may be able to determine with certainty is that the man's feeling of relaxation is not overcome by the competing feeling of having to get away. After sex, a man may be incapable of communicating anything, good or bad. And here's where our Maker played another trick on us. After sex, a woman typically feels incredibly alert, talkative, intimate, ready to cuddle and laugh. After sex, a man is either a zombie or dead. How should we handle this impossible situation? Know this: We understand that a woman needs intimacy. So do we! But immediately after ejaculation is *not* the time for a heart-to-heart talk.

If he stays the night, be happy that he wants to, but understand that when a woman attempts to force a man to stay awake it is like the torture tactics that the enemy uses on a prisoner of war. We have all had the experience of a woman complaining about a man falling asleep after sex instead of talking or cuddling. A woman becomes insulted and thinks that the man is doing this because he does not care. It has nothing to do with caring or not caring. It is just an involuntary physical response. Don't take it personally. Don't torture him. Just give him a reassuring kiss good night and let him rest.

Brad recalls an evening when he engaged in sexual intercourse with a woman. After they had finished, Brad immediately fell asleep. The sex was tiring, he had had a long day at work, had gone to the gym, had written a chapter of this book, and had finished the evening at this woman's apartment. He just wanted to fall into a sound sleep. The woman had a different idea. She attempted to engage him in conversation. When she noticed he was sleeping, she began yelling at him. Brad lied to her and said he was awake. He stated that he was just "resting his eyes." He began to fall in and out of consciousness during her conversation. Every minute or two he would wake up and say a word or two to make it seem as if he was listening and then he would nod off again. She literally would not let him sleep. She took Brad's reaction personally when he really couldn't help it. Brad remembered her conduct, and it made it difficult for him to see her again. He feared that she would torture him if he stayed over at her apartment.

Do you know about a man's refractory period? We suspect that only a few of you actually know what we are talking about because every time we mention this topic to a woman we get a puzzled look. The refractory period is the period of time after a man has an orgasm until the time he is physically ready to do it again. After a man has an orgasm, his penis is out of commission. It doesn't matter if you are Cindy Crawford or Pamela Anderson. A man's penis is limp. Nothing will revive it, and it is very sensitive to the touch. We suggest that you don't even think about trying to get things working again. For each man the refractory period is different. Some men need hours to recover, others need minutes. There is really nothing you can do to speed up the process. As a matter of fact, anything that you do could slow it down. Don't take it personally. It has no bearing on how sexually attracted he is to you. It is purely physical. Just give your man time.

Now you know everything you need to know about men and sex. You might even know too much. We admit that an inside view of men's sexuality is not for the fainthearted. And we hope other men won't hold it against us for letting women in on our sexual secrets, and worse, for cautioning women to use sexual discretion early in the game. But we do think it crucial that more women know the nitty-gritty of men's desire. Women need to know because, for men, sexual compatibility is almost everything.

Remember, at the beginning of a relationship: *Practice sexual caution!*

When the two of you have established intimacy:

Use your sexual power!

Don't be shy, tell him how to please you. Talk to him!

Be open to trying out new things in new places!

And, after ejaculation, hands off. A man needs his shut-eye, and most professional men are sleep deprived.

Nine

~~~~~~

THE RELATIONSHIP, PART I:
PRACTICAL ISSUES

Sexual compatibility is essential, and deep emotional issues are important to work through, but they are not the only things that get in the way of happiness in love. Let's talk about those day-in and day-out issues that strain even the most loving of relationships. Some aspects of "guyness" seem to bug women no end. Our aim here is to show you a man's point of view on some common "thorns" in women's sides so you don't let them cut deeply into the heart of your relationship.

Guys' Night Out

We need to spend time with other men. Male bonding is one of the most cherished rituals for any professional man. All through his childhood, a male is taught to be "one of the guys." His father and male friends tell him to "be a man," to "go out for the team," to "toughen up." He is ridiculed when he doesn't conform to these outside pressures. His friends taunt him with names like "loser," "wimp," or "pussy." Such name-calling among friends is not really intended to cast him out of the male group. Its purpose is to reinforce the male attitude. In fact, this name-calling is part of "being a man." Camaraderie between men develops in childhood, continues through adulthood, and our fathers have told us it continues into old age. Male bonding is ingrained in our psyches. It is something that we need in order to survive as men.

Therefore, it should not come as a surprise to you when we say that *we need to go out with the guys*. When a professional man is in a committed relationship with a woman, he spends less time with his friends than before he met her. He is spending more time with the woman he loves and he may even neglect his friends. This is when his good old buddies start doing what they have been taught to do since childhood: They ridicule him for spending all of his free time with his girlfriend. They call him "lover boy" and teasingly suggest that he may be "pussy whipped." Are they doing this because they don't like him anymore? Of course not. They are doing it because they miss hanging out with him. Men often show affection for one another by trading insults. If a man's friends don't ridicule him, then they probably didn't like him in the first place. Professional men enjoy this camaraderie because it makes them feel like they are "one of the guys."

So when a man says he wants to hang out with the guys one night, it means more to him than just a simple night out. It is his time to be alone with the guys, to be a man among men. You may be asking yourself what "being a man among men" means. It means talking about work, reminiscing about the good old days when you were single, being rude, talking about sports, or talking about this girl's ass and that girl's breasts. Men sometimes even talk about their bodily functions in such great detail that it would make most women sick. It's our time to be immature—to be with the boys again.

Now, we are not saying that a man should spend all his free time with his friends. We are saying that he needs to keep in contact with his friends and go out with them on occasion. Giving him a hard time about this, or prohibiting him from seeing his friends, can put a *major* strain on the relationship. If you appreciate how important a man's friends are to him, in his eyes you will be a "cool" and understanding woman. If you can let go of him in this way, *it will bring him closer to you*. But beware: If he is spending more time with his friends than he is with you, this may be a sign that there is a problem—he is losing interest in the relationship.

There are some things that every woman needs to know about "guys' night out." First of all, *never* ask to go along. Bringing a girlfriend to "guys' night out" will incur more ridicule than if he hadn't gone at all and instead had spent the day with you at the local flower show. Having girlfriends at "guys' night out" is one of the ultimate signs of being "whipped." It also changes the dynamics of the entire evening. Your boyfriend is now concerned about you and how you are enjoying your night. This takes him away from talking to his friends. The other men in the group are also inhibited in their conversation with one another because a woman is present. In short, it is no longer "guys' night out." It is now "guys' night out with their buddy and his girlfriend"—truly *not* a male-bonding experience. If a man's girlfriend persists in always tagging along on "guys' night out," his friends may even begin to resent her because she is disrupting their precious male-bonding time. If she lets her boyfriend spend time alone with his friends, both he and his friends will respect her for this.

One night Rich went out with the guys after work. His girlfriend, Marla, also went out with her friends to the same bar. They had planned to hang out with their respective friends and go home together at the end of the night. While Rich and his male friends were venting about work and ranting about sports, Marla came over to say hello. Immediately the "guy talk" stopped. The dynamics of the conversation underwent that seismic shift that sometimes happens when a woman enters an exclusively male group. While Marla was standing there with Rich and the guys, Rich began to feel more and more uncomfortable. Rich then told Marla how important it was for him to be alone with his friends. She understood and went back to her friends. Rich stopped sweating and started realizing how special Marla was for understanding him. His friends even commented on how "cool" she was for letting the guys hang out alone. Later that night when they met up, Rich told Marla how much it meant to him that she let the guys "be guys." By leaving Rich alone with his friends, Marla brought herself closer to Rich's heart.

A lot of women think that when their boyfriends go out with the guys they are looking to meet other women. We hope by now that you understand this is not a "scam session," he is just hanging out with his friends. On those evenings when he is with his friends and not you, he is not looking to score a one-night stand with a willing stranger.

In fact, when a professional man comes home after a night out with his friends, he will have a renewed feeling of love for his girlfriend. After being in the company of other men, he is ready for that very special and different feeling of being with the woman he loves. And he loves her more for understanding his need to be with his friends. The worst thing you can do when your boyfriend comes home from a night out without you is to subject him to the third-degree and grill him with questions about his night. This makes him think that you don't trust him or understand him and *it will distance him from you.*

Guys' Night Out Deluxe: The Bachelor Party

There are some times when "guys' night out" is especially important to a man, and extrasensitive for a woman. A bachelor party for the soon-to-be-married buddy is one of those times. A surefire way to start an argument and cause a strain on your relationship is to give your boyfriend a hard time about going, or even worse, say that he can't go. Let us explain.

The bachelor party is probably the most sacred "guys' night out" to most men. This is a time when a man's friends can give him his last hurrah. It is a rite of passage for all men who will be losing their single life and gaining a beautiful bride. The bachelor party is the ultimate male-bonding experience. Every man wants to have one and every man wants to go to one. And every man is expected to attend if invited. In fact, it is a sign of disrespect when a man does not go to his friend's bachelor party. Skipping this very important event will not only provoke ridicule from the groom and the other friends, they will have real feelings of ill will toward your boyfriend. Think of how you would feel if one of your friends did not go to your bridal shower. Wouldn't you be upset if your friend did not come to share this special day with you? Well, it's just as important for a man to attend his buddy's bachelor party.

It's true that most women would not approve of what goes on at bachelor parties. We will not be drinking milk and eating cookies, and we will not be playing pin the tail on the donkey. There will probably be strippers, porno films, and a lot of booze. The thing you must ask yourself when your boyfriend goes to a bachelor party is: Are we in a trusting relationship or not? If the answer is no, then you shouldn't be in the relationship in the first place. If the answer is yes, as it probably is, then you should let him go without any hassles because you will have nothing to worry about. It will show him that you understand how important the bachelor party is for the groom. It will also show that you trust him and, as a result, *he will respect you and appreciate you even more.*

Guys' Night Out Galore: The Strip Bar

Another special "guys' night out" is a trip to the strip bar. This is a night when men can get together and do one of the things they are genetically programmed to do—gawk at women. Going to a strip bar is a pastime that every man enjoys no matter what his profession or age. Your boyfriend, husband, brother, uncle, father, and grandfather have been to one. In fact, the chances are that they have visited one more than once. A night out at the strip bar is another one of those male-bonding experiences.

We understand that a lot of women feel uncomfortable about having their boyfriends go to strip bars. Does it mean that he doesn't love you anymore or that he doesn't think you are attractive? No. To a man, a strip bar is a taste of a life that he can't have. Having an unknown topless woman approach him, be nice, and then seductively dance for him is every man's fantasy. This has to do with a man's insecurities. After all of those years of approaching women, being turned down, and being frustrated, it is nice to have the tables turned and have a beautiful woman approach him. This is a definite ego boost for him, and it does not necessarily mean that anything is wrong with your relationship.

Men also need variety in their lives. As we've said, if his woman is tall and blond, he will stare at that pretty petite brunette as if he'd just gotten out of prison. Looking at different women satisfies his visual imagination. When men enter a strip bar, they are not thinking to themselves, "I am going to have sex with one of these women tonight." They just like to look at naked women.

Understanding a man's desire to go to a strip bar will improve your relationship with your boyfriend. First of all, professional men think it is "cool" when their girlfriends do not have a problem with their going. It shows that you are secure about yourself and your relationship, and *you will look better in his eyes*. Second, we are horny when we get home. So if you don't get upset about where he spent the evening and instead wear a sexy negligee when he walks in the door, you can turn what would have been a disappointing evening into an exciting night. Instead of shunning him, welcome him and *you will be assured of an incredible lovemaking session*.

Guys Just Being Guys: Watching the Game

Another favorite male pastime, as probably all of you women know, is watching sports. Professional men love to watch sports. We are not trying to ignore you. We are not trying to annoy you. We just love sports. It stems from our childhood years in the playground or on the playing field. Every boy who has ever played a sport has dreamed of hitting the winning home run in the ninth inning of the last game of the World Series, making the winning shot at the buzzer in the NBA playoffs, or scoring the winning touchdown in the final seconds of the Super Bowl. Men rarely fulfill these dreams. Instead, we root for the home team and share in their glory.

The game is important to us. We like to watch it without interruption. And more important for you, *a professional man will appreciate you* if you let him watch it. A sympathetic woman may even delay day or evening plans with a man so he can watch a game that is important to him. Believe us—it will pay great dividends!

For example, Rich really wanted to watch a Giants-Eagles football game one Sunday. These are both his favorite teams and watching the game meant a lot to him. Marla wanted to go to the mall to pick out a vase for her apartment. Marla understood how important the game was to him, and stayed in and watched it with him although she is certainly not a die-hard football fan. He was so appreciative of her understanding and her willingness to stay with him that he took her to the flower show in town and bought her a dozen roses as well as the vase she wanted. Yes, Rich did actually go to a flower show.

Professional men do like it when their girlfriends watch sports with them. Note we said *watch*. Trying to initiate in-depth discussions during the game is a bad move and will most probably cause an argument. If you can't watch the game without trying to talk to your boyfriend, then it is probably better to let him watch it alone. He is focusing his full attention on the game. He is not ignoring you on purpose. Remember, he is living out those childhood fantasies and sharing in the glory of victory or the agony of defeat.

Double-Dating Dilemmas

Many women may not know that men view double-dating with their girlfriend's friends very differently than double-dating with their own friends. To a professional man, a double date with his girlfriend's friends is less like a date and more like a chore. There are two reasons for a man's apprehension. First, men don't like meeting other men for the first time in this way. Male friendships usually begin on the basketball court, in the locker room, at work, or on a hunting or hiking trip. These are the situations in which men can bond and form friendships. Meeting a guy for the first time and not being able to "be a guy" because there are ladies present is, frankly, an awkward situation for a man. Yes, your boyfriend will make polite small talk, but he is not really enjoying it. He is counting the seconds as they go by and hoping that the fire alarm goes off in the restaurant so that the night can end early.

Second, we feel as though we have to be on our best behavior because we are going to be judged by your friends. We have to watch what we say and do. We also have to make sure that we are paying enough attention to you, to your friend, and to her date. If we are lucky, we can manage to enjoy the meal. There is too much pressure placed on us for this to be a pleasant experience.

But we do it anyway because we know it means a lot to you. So, if at all possible, try to make the night easier for us. It is helpful for us to know what type of relationship you have with your friend and what her background is. Are you high school friends? Acquaintances from work? Maybe she is your aerobics instructor? Also, tell us about your friend's date: What's his profession? What's he like? What is his relationship with your friend? All of this information will give us ammunition for those deadly silences when everyone is staring at their plates and hoping someone will say something. One of the most humane things you can do is end the double date early if you see that your boyfriend is having a terrible time. Believe us, we have all been in this situation and wished someone had shown us some sympathy.

On the other hand, men feel much more comfortable going on double dates with their friends. This is true because there is no chance that the awkward male-male tension will develop or that we will fear that our every move will be judged. As a result, we will be much happier on these double dates. It gives us a chance to male-bond a little and also be with the woman we care about.

For some men, double-dating with his friends and you may even replace "guys' night out." One of our friends started a new job and his hours were crazy. He was involved in a relationship with a woman he loved very much. We didn't get to see him that often because of his hectic schedule. His girlfriend also didn't get to spend as much time with him as she would have liked. This is a perfect situation in which a double date with the man's friends can replace "guys' night out." It gives the guys a chance to male-bond a little and also enjoy a night out with their girlfriends. In a professional man's mind, this is the best of both worlds.

In these situations, though, guys like to be involved in some male conversations, such as discussing sports, the gym, or work. So we like it when our dates are able to talk with our friends' dates while we are catching up. This shows that you are an independent woman and do not constantly need a man's attention. These are two *important qualities that a professional man finds very attractive in a woman*. We are not saying that it's okay for a man to ignore his girlfriend all night. In fact, this is very rude, and you should confront your boyfriend when he does this. But, if he is catching up with his friends, then let him do so. *He will appreciate your independent spirit.*

Dealing with His Friends

Getting serious with him does mean dealing with his friends. There's no way around it. Your relationship with them can determine how successful and happy your relationship with him will ultimately be. Most men will have a group of two or three very close friends and a larger group of acquaintances. It is important for you to befriend his close buddies because they are the ones, besides you, to whom he will look for support and reinforcement.

He will look to see how you mingle with his friends. If you can't make conversation with them, he may think, What's up with her? and start wondering about how compatible you are with him. Making enemies of your boyfriend's friends will create a major strain on the relationship. We are not saying that a relationship will end because a man's girlfriend doesn't like his friends, or they don't like her, but it is one of those things that he hopes won't happen. If it does, he will have to compartmentalize his life: He will have to choose between his friends and the woman he loves. A professional man wants a woman who likes his friends so that he can take her out with them on special occasions and double dates. When a man's girlfriend gets along with his friends, or at least tolerates them, he will be thankful.

The best way to strike up a good relationship with your boyfriend's friends is not to let yourself be threatened by them. A man needs the company of men as well as the company of the woman he loves. Understand his need for male bonding and let your boyfriend do it every now and then. His friends will like you for being such a cool chick and he will admire you for understanding his needs.

Keeping Up with the Joneses

Many women try to compare their relationships with their friends' relationships. Professional men hate this. We often wonder why women do it. When a man knows that he has been compared to another man, or your relationship has been compared to another one, he thinks you think he is not good enough for you. This fosters a man's insecurities. Essentially, you are saying to him, "Why can't you be more like him?" or "Why can't you love me as much as he loves her?" These can be very damaging questions. How would you feel if your boyfriend compared you to another woman in this way?

The bottom line is that we feel resentful and hurt when we are negatively compared to other men by our loved ones. Doing this will probably cause your boyfriend to either clam up and not talk to you or lash out and start a fight. It will certainly not make him say, "Okay, I will stop being myself now and be more like this other guy." Any comparisons with other men will hinder or halt the dialogue you need to resolve the issue that concerns you. The best way to deal with any problems in your relationship is to confront your boyfriend without getting angry. Talk to him about what you need and want from him in a relationship. You will *reap much greater rewards* with this tactic.

Family Matters

Introducing a woman to his parents is a big moment for a professional man. If a man is willing to do this, he certainly views the relationship as serious. In fact, it is a big deal for a man to even discuss his family in depth or talk about "family issues." If he does this, it is a sure sign that he *respects you and values your opinion* and is willing to "step up" the relationship and *bring you closer to his heart*.

This is such a serious issue for a man because he usually respects his family and their views of him very much. If a man does not think a woman he is dating is "wife material," then he will definitely not introduce her to his family. He does not want his family to say to him, "Why are you going out with her?" or "You can do better than her," or "She's not the one for you." The possibility of hearing such harsh comments is always in the back of a man's mind when he considers taking a woman home to meet his parents.

There are a few reasons that a man you have been dating for a while may not ask you to meet his parents: He does not see you as a potential wife, he is not close to his parents or his parents are deceased, or he is holding off for now because he is not ready to "step up" the relationship. It can take a man up to six months of dating a woman before he makes the decision to introduce her to his parents. If six months have gone by and you still have not met his parents, we suggest that you gently raise the issue. You might simply say, "I would really like to meet your parents, they sound like such nice people," or "Tell me more about your family, I want to know what it was like for you growing up." If he cares about you, then he will understand that this is important to you and will make the necessary introductions. If he still does not introduce you after you have expressed your interest, and he has a good relationship with his parents, then you can be assured that he has no intention of ever introducing you. At this point it is time to move on if you are looking for a serious, long-term commitment.

On the brighter side, if he does ask you to meet his parents, then he considers you "wife material." This does not mean that he is immediately going to go out and buy you a ring, but you will know that you are in the running.

A woman should keep a few things in mind when she meets her boyfriend's parents. First of all, don't take this event lightly. Your first meeting with his parents is especially crucial—it can even make or break a relationship. If a professional man is close to his family, he will seek approval from them. It is a good idea to get on his parents' good side early on. Do your best to get along with his mother. This might not be easy. A bad scenario is when a man's girlfriend and his mother clash. If this happens, he will worry that if he marries this woman, he will have to deal with the extreme tension and hassles that are created every time the two women he loves the most get together. Relationships are difficult enough without dealing with this added tension. A professional man might consider a woman "non-wife material" after seeing an obvious rift develop between his parents and his girlfriend.

A woman will greatly benefit when she is liked by her boyfriend's parents. How will she benefit? His parents will put pressure on their son to stay in the relationship with her. They may even try to pressure him into marrying her. So if you are interested in marrying your boyfriend, do your best to win his parents over and *never* be rude or disrespectful toward them—even if you are pushed to the limit.

For a professional man, meeting his girlfriend's family is a stressful situation as well. He will be on his best behavior and may not even seem like the guy you know. He is being especially nice because, in his mind, meeting the parents is a big deal. If he cares about your feelings, he will respect your parents.

It is a good idea to brief your boyfriend about your family before the meeting. Which family member is the most important to you? Who is the most difficult to get along with? Which topics should he definitely not discuss? What are your family members' individual interests? You should provide him with the answers to these questions to help his meeting with your family go smoothly.

A man is most nervous when meeting his girlfriend's father. You know why. Fathers scrutinize the men who are pursuing their daughters. Your boyfriend knows that your dad was once single and knows how guys act. In your boyfriend's mind, your father is looking at him and through him, trying to see if he is worthy of his daughter. Your boyfriend will discreetly try to bond with your father. You will help him do this by giving him information about your father's job, hobbies, and likes and dislikes.

When a professional man meets his girlfriend's mom, he is more at ease. We believe that women talk to their mothers more about their boyfriends and relationships, so it seems as if the mothers know us pretty thoroughly before we even meet them. This makes the meeting go a lot more smoothly. We can also turn on our charm a bit with our girlfriend's mother. This helps ease the tension for us. Be aware that any negative comments you might have made to your mother about your boyfriend will add a lot of tension to the meeting. This usually happens after you have had a fight with him. You should at least tell him about this or try to smooth things over with your mother before the meeting.

A guy will do his best to befriend his girlfriend's brother. He will try to bond with him as he did with the father. A man always expects his girlfriend's brother to be on the defensive during the first meeting because brothers know how men think. The brother will look out for his sister and try to make sure she will not be hurt or used by her boyfriend. Sometimes there may be some competition between them.

Chris was once in a serious relationship with a woman who had a brother his age. There was a lot of competition between the two men. Everything Chris did, the brother tried to do better. Chris was uncomfortable, and it put a strain on his relationship with his girlfriend. Rich, in contrast, gets along well with Marla's brother. They have similar viewpoints about many issues, and there is absolutely no competition between them. The two men have formed a friendship, and this enhances the relationship between Rich and Marla.

Vacationing Together

Like meeting the family, deciding to vacation together marks a big step in the relationship. To spend essentially every second of a week or two alone with his girlfriend in a new and foreign place is a very ominous prospect for most men, especially when it's the first time. This is true no matter how much he loves you or how close the two of you are. For this reason, every man is apprehensive about going on a vacation with his girlfriend for the first time.

At this point in the relationship, he has probably never spent the amount of time or paid the amount of attention to you that would be required during a vacation. He will think to himself that every time he gets up in the morning, brushes his teeth, eats breakfast, lunch, and dinner, goes out at night, and goes to sleep, you will be there. Not that this is a bad thing, but he just does not know how he will be able to handle it. This is why he is apprehensive about going on vacation with you. It can take a man a year or more before he is comfortable with going on a vacation with his girlfriend.

When you do decide to go on a vacation together, it is a good idea to plan it together. You should plan a vacation both of you will be able to enjoy—this may require some compromise—or else the vacation is destined to be a horrible experience. When Rich and Marla first went on an extended vacation together, Rich had all of the apprehensions just described. They had been on many smaller weekend getaways together and had had a great time, but the big vacation hadn't yet happened, mostly because of Rich's apprehension (and busy schedule). Rich knew that he had a great time on vacation with Brad and Chris, running with the bulls in Spain and visiting the Greek islands. Would he have as much fun with his girlfriend?

Well, it took about a year and a half before Rich overcame his apprehensions. They decided to take a domestic trip for their first vacation. They both sat down and carefully planned what they wanted to do and where they wanted to go. Rich and Marla enjoyed a trip that was fun and romantic for both of them and, as a result, became even closer. It was well worth the wait. If they had gone sooner, before Rich was ready, then it probably would have been a disaster and could have hurt their relationship.

We recommend holding off on vacationing together until you are in a committed relationship. Spending too much time together before you really know each other can be awkward and can derail a promising relationship. If you do go on vacation together, realize what a man's fears are. He worries that you will require too much attention. He also worries that he will not be able to "be himself." Being relaxed and self-sufficient will go a long way toward making your vacation together a pleasure, not an ordeal.

Presents, Presents

Buying gifts for a woman can be one of the most difficult and painful experiences for a professional man. A man will try to buy the perfect gift for the woman he loves. Unfortunately, he knows that his idea of a perfect gift is far from his girlfriend's idea of a perfect gift. So when he is looking for that special gift, he must try to think like a woman. This is where most of the frustration comes into play. A man does not like to think like a woman, nor is he capable of doing it at all well. He will become confused and uncomfortable. He might even ask his sister or mother for some help in getting him through this experience.

The search for a perfect gift can take weeks of going to boutiques, little crafts shops, large department stores, and women's apparel stores. We can think of plenty of places a man would rather spend his free time. Even though this is an ordeal for us, we do it anyway because we care about the woman in our lives and we know it means a lot to her. So when it is time for your boyfriend to buy you a gift, try to understand the tremendous job he has ahead. Subtle hints are very helpful and can ease some of the tension headaches that may arise.

When the moment of truth comes and you open that gift, try to remember the time and effort that he spent in search of it. Whatever the gift may be, the worst thing you can do is show immediate disappointment. This will hurt his feelings and will probably make him resent you. Joking or making fun of the gift is not a good idea either—remember, his mother could have helped him pick it out.

If you want to avoid hurting his feelings, and ensure that you receive a better gift the next time, forget about the bad gift you just got and *give him help* when it's time for the next gift-giving opportunity. Before you know it, the bread maker you got last Valentine's Day will turn into gorgeous heart-shaped earrings this year.

When the three of us went to Spain a few years ago, Brad needed to buy a gift for his girlfriend. He spent many hours at different outdoor markets, gift shops, and boutiques, but ended up frustrated each time he tried to find that "perfect gift." It got to the point where our vacation plans were revolving around the local shopping districts. By the end of the trip, Brad still had not found anything for his girlfriend. In an act of desperation, he went into a Body Shop at the Madrid airport and bought her an assortment of soap. Admittedly, it was not the perfect gift, but it was something he thought she would like. When he gave it to her, he could immediately see her disappointment on her face. This hurt his feelings, and he resented her for it. He couldn't believe how unappreciative she was after all that time and effort he'd spent searching.

For a man, accepting a gift is a much more pleasurable experience than finding one to give. A man appreciates any gift a woman gives him. It certainly does not have to be big or expensive—although it is okay when it is. We like the thought and creativeness that women put into selecting gifts for us.

We think that it is easier for a woman to shop for a man than it is for a man to shop for a woman. To a man, your gift is seen purely as a token of your appreciation. So when you give him that nice paperweight for his desk at work, he is not saying to himself, "This gift sucks! I wish she'd gotten me that leather briefcase that I've always wanted." He may have really wanted that briefcase, but he will appreciate the paperweight because it came from the woman he loves. This is not to say that he wouldn't be jumping up and down if you got him that leather briefcase. Yes, he does want it more, and yes, he would have liked that gift better than the paperweight. But, he does like the fact that you thought of him in some way. If you really want to give him a gift he will really like but are not sure what to get, then ask him what he wants or even take him shopping for that gift. This is one situation in which professional men don't mind going shopping.

Giving a gift that he will especially like is important because he will brag to his parents and friends about the wonderful gift you gave him. This will *make you look good in the eyes of the people who care about him*. If they see that you are getting him nice gifts and making him especially happy, then they will like you in return. This can only *enhance your relationship* with your boyfriend.

The Domestic Woman

In these times of female independence and equality, men sometimes miss the domestic woman. This does not mean that we prefer her. The professional man would much rather be with a woman who has her own career, ideas, and aspirations. We do like it, though, when our independent, career-oriented girlfriends show a *small* amount of domesticity.

The truth is, men love to be nurtured and taken care of by

women. Men like it when the women they love can do some of the "domestic female things" that our mothers, grandmothers, and great-grandmothers did for their husbands. We are not talking about churning butter or making a quilt. We like little things, such as having a home-cooked meal prepared for us or having our bed made in the morning.

There are more ways to a man's heart than through his stomach, but a professional man really does appreciate a home-cooked meal. It means a number of things to him. It shows him that his girlfriend cares enough to take the extra time to cook for him. He is relieved that he does not have to eat the same old take-out meal again. And, it brings back memories of all the times his mother fed him as a child. As a result of this one meal that his girlfriend prepared, he feels appreciated, relieved, and nostalgic. The home-cooked meal *will definitely bring your boyfriend closer to you.*

Professional men don't want their girlfriends to be their maids, but they greatly appreciate their doing the little things that they wouldn't normally do for themselves. If you do these little things once in a while, it will show that you care about your boyfriend and that you care about taking care of him. For example, Chris was seriously dating a girl with certain domestic virtues. After arriving at his apartment, she would be there for ten minutes and during their conversation about their day or what was new in their lives, almost without his noticing, she would tidy the place up a bit. No major cleaning like vacuuming or washing the windows, just some little things done around the apartment that made the place look better in two minutes. Chris greatly appreciated it, and it didn't take much for her to do it. Straightening out his messy apartment is a gift you can give that takes a minimum of effort.

Another little thing that you can do that your boyfriend will really like is to make his bed for him in the morning.

Men rarely make their beds. To a man this seems like a waste of time. He is thinking, "Why should I make it if I am just going to mess it up tonight?" But, when he sees that his girlfriend has made it for him, he immediately thinks of her. He knows that she has put her womanly touch on the place where he sleeps every night. It is like a small, special gift to him. He will think of her during his day, and he will think about getting in that bed with her later that night.

Professional women may struggle with this and find it hard to allow themselves to do such things. It may be a matter of principle. We respect your judgment in this and we don't want you to think we are suggesting any kind of slave labor or anything. All we are saying is that it is nice to have a woman's touch around the apartment. Don't you appreciate it when we help you move a bookcase, pick you up at the airport, or fix your VCR?

The Black Book

You know it is sitting around somewhere and you hate the fact that he has not thrown it away. Yes, it is the infamous "black book." The black book is a professional man's special "scrapbook" that only he can understand and appreciate. It is like a security blanket for him. It reminds him of the days when he was single and sought after by different women. It is a part of his history, his life, and his manhood. Needless to say, this little book, with the names of women in his past who have probably moved, and phone numbers that have most probably been disconnected, is important to him.

He is not going to use it to try to contact these women. It is probably useless for this function. When he is in one of those melancholic and nostalgic moods, he may look at it to make himself feel better. You may experience a similar feeling when you flip through old photo albums and look at pictures of your former self and your past boyfriends. These are special, private moments that only you can really appreciate. You have a chance to look back at your life as only you can. No one else can understand how you feel when you look at your photo albums. More important, no one else can understand how important these personal pictures are to you.

This is how we feel about the black book. We know that there is no way you can understand how we feel when we look at the black book. It is odd, but there is a feeling of security in just knowing that it still exists and is stored away in a safe place. It is difficult for us to understand why this is true, so we don't expect you to understand it either.

All we can ask is that you understand how important the black book is to him. An obvious negative thing for you to do is to tell him to throw it away or belittle him for keeping it. The best way to handle this situation is to not bring up the subject and let things happen naturally. There will come a time when he will voluntarily throw it away, but he must be ready. Throwing away the black book will be one of his last symbolic gestures of total commitment to you, and marriage will not be far away.

A man's attachment to his little black book is part of deep-structure "guyness." So is his need to be out with the guys, his sports fanaticism, his craving for staring at a variety of naked women, and his gift-shopping panic. We are not trying to irritate or hurt women when we do these things. We are just being guys. It helps when women understand this. When women understand that there are some things men cannot change, the course of love runs more smoothly.

Ten

THE RELATIONSHIP, PART II:
THE ART OF LOVING

Those Romantic Moments . . .

Picture yourself on a moonlit beach with your lover. You share a bottle of wine, talking and touching softly. The stars are shining brightly and the ocean is glistening from the reflection of the moon and the stars. You hear the rhythmic crash of waves on the shoreline. There is meaning in the look in his eyes and in the way he touches your face.

Now picture yourself in a dark, candlelit restaurant. You and he are seated at a table for two, oblivious to the world around you. The candles on your table have melted halfway down and the waiter has just poured you the last glass of Pinot Grigio. You are not even speaking, just gazing into each other's eyes. He slowly reaches across the table and gently places his hand over yours. You feel as if you are going to melt inside.

Why Doesn't He Enjoy Romantic Moments As Much As You Do?

These are some of your most intimate moments with your boyfriend. It was probably not difficult for you to paint these pictures in your mind. Imagining them probably made you feel warm inside and brought a smile to your face. Well, these pictures are extremely hard for a man to paint in his mind and they usually don't bring a smile to his face. In fact, they make him cringe. Although some men may occasionally enjoy times like these, many men could do without them. It is very difficult for a man to be so romantic. It goes against his grain. This does not mean that he loves you any less. It is just a man's nature. All of those years of roughhousing as a boy and the everyday pressure to be one of the guys have trained a man to not feel this way.

We do understand how important romance can be to a woman. However, *men do not like it when their girlfriends try to force them into being romantic*. Romance is not something that can be forced—it must come from within and be brought out naturally. It is hard for people to be what they are not. If a moment of emotional intimacy feels too forced or fake, a man will resist it. A man may respond favorably to a hint. You can smile and say, "You know I love to receive a card, or a flower, from you." But you should not measure how much your boyfriend loves you by how romantic he is. He may love you very much but may not be romantic. Forcing him to be romantic can foster his insecurity. If he sees that you are not happy with how he expresses his love for you, he may feel that you think he is not good enough for you. This will undoubtedly put a strain on the relationship.

If romance is extremely important to you, and your boyfriend is not romantic enough for you, then it may be time for you to make a decision. This may be a clear sign that the two of you may not be compatible. Don't think it is going to change. Continuously trying to force it out of your boyfriend will be a hardship on the relationship. If it is something you need and want, then you should not settle for anything less. If you do settle, it will eventually catch up with you in the long run and make you unhappy. Our advice is to move on, as hard as it may seem. If you are constantly exasperated that he is not romantic enough, then the relationship will be doomed.

And Why Doesn't He Say "I Love You"?

Saying "I love you" is also difficult for some men. This is especially true the first time a man declares himself to a particular woman. It is a major decision for a man to tell a woman that he loves her. It weighs on his mind for a long time and he thinks it over very carefully before saying it. There are some men who find it so difficult to say that they will avoid saying it. They think the guys will make fun of them if they find out they told their girlfriends they love them. It is another one of those macho things in which the testosterone level alters the way of thinking.

We do know how important it is to you for your boyfriend to tell you he loves you. If you are in a relationship where you are in love and you believe he loves you, there are certain things you can do to speed up his declaration without causing any harm. You might initiate casual talk about how close you have become, how much you enjoy each other's company, and how terrific the relationship is. Pick your time carefully, though. Bringing it up in the ninth inning of game six of the World Series when the Yankees are about to win the championship would not be an ideal time.

Subtle conversations like this serve two purposes. The first is to provide your boyfriend with a wake-up call and make him realize how deep the relationship has become. Remember, professional men have a lot going on in their lives and they don't like to analyze or pay attention to things that appear to be going well. They are so used to putting out fires at work and dealing with everyday stress that if their relationships with their girlfriends are going well, they feel there is no need to tend to them. Relationships tend to progress on cruise control in these circumstances. Second, after a few hints about the topic, he will have the necessary information to know that if and when he says those three magic words, you will say them back.

A professional man's biggest fear is losing his manhood. If he tells you he loves you and you do not say it back, he will feel that his biggest fear has become truth. He has decided to tell you the one thing that is most difficult for him to say. Before he tells you he will ask himself, What happens if she says "Oh, that's so sweet!" or "Really? I never knew you felt that way" or "That's nice and I like you too"? The responses that he will run through his mind are endless. For him, there is one and only one sufficient response to his telling you that he loves you: your saying "I love you too." Anything short of this will crush his ego and make him more insecure than ever. You might as well call a psychiatric hospital and have him admitted, because if he doesn't hear "I love you" back, he is going to go crazy.

He will tell himself over and over that he shouldn't have said it. He will kick himself and ask himself what the hell he was thinking. When the smoke clears and he has finished beating himself up over why he decided to do such a stupid thing, the mental problems will begin. He will wonder why you didn't say it back. He will feel insecure, inadequate, and unloved. He will wonder how he allowed the relationship to get to a point where he loved you yet you didn't love him. He will say things to himself like "Where did I go wrong? This isn't supposed to happen. It's the woman who is supposed to fall in love first, not the man. What's wrong with me? And more important, how do I regain my dignity with her?" As you can see, he is now even more screwed up than he was before his brilliant move.

Now you know why it is such a major step for your boyfriend to tell you he loves you, and why it takes so long. Those preliminary conversations will put his mind at ease so that he knows that when he does say it, you will say it back. If a man loves you, he will eventually tell you so. But encouraging words that reinforce rather than demand will work wonders to speed up his declaration of love.

We strongly suggest that you *not* say "I love you" before a man has declared himself. There are good reasons for this. It seems to us that women, on the average, fall in love faster than men. Once a woman falls in love, she may want to tell her boyfriend that she loves him. Although men like to hear it, they only like to hear it if they also love the woman. If you tell your boyfriend that you love him, and he doesn't love you, he will immediately feel guilty. Yes, men do feel guilt. If you declare your love for him, and he is noncommittal or uncertain, he will immediately go into a state of panic. He knows he has only a matter of seconds to react. But this is not like that split-second decision he has to make while playing in a football game or while buying and selling stocks. This is a whole different type of panic. For him, it's a kind of death: His whole life flashes before his eyes in a matter of seconds. This is what happens to a man when a woman says "I love you" and he doesn't love her.

Men know that women need to hear that positive response just as they do, and that it has to be quick. Love is not something that you think about for a minute or two and then decide to declare. It is something that you feel deep down, and if you do love somebody, you should be able to tell them so as soon as they tell you. So what happens? Well, in this state of panic, the only thing he can do is say it back whether he loves you or not. Not saying it back would just open up a can of worms, and a deep talk about the relationship would immediately ensue. What guy wants to deal with that? If he is really interested in you but doesn't love you yet, he will fear losing you or upsetting you. To cover his panic and fear he would rather just say it and live with the possible later consequences.

However, those consequences tend to be severe. Almost immediately he realizes that he is living a lie. He begins to feel uncomfortable and pressured. Since men are not good emotional communicators, he will allow this to fester. It will cause an incredible strain on him to see you, knowing that he has told you he loves you when he really doesn't. Now the relationship is headed for trouble. *Take our advice, let him say "I love you" first.*

Once you get past the milestone of declaring your love for each other, another hurdle must be jumped. It seems that women enjoy repeated verbal declarations of love. Our Maker played another little game on us by making men women's exact opposites in this respect. Men don't like to say "I love you" repeatedly. In fact, we know some men who never say it. It seems strange, we know, but even if your boyfriend loves you with all his heart, sometimes he may feel self-conscious saying it out loud. We do not recommend pressuring him into saying "I love you" more often. The more you ask to hear it, the less you will hear it. The more pressure you bring to bear, the more he will withdraw—and then you will end up in a fight.

Remember, men are not good emotional communicators. If we are bad at saying "I love you" in private, we are terrible at it if asked to say it in public. Don't put your boyfriend in a situation where you pressure him into saying "I love you" in front of his friends. This will embarrass him. We are sure you have had that dream in which you are at school or at work and you are standing there either naked or in your under-wear. Well, asking your boyfriend to say "I love you" in front of his friends is like putting him in his office in his underwear. Remember, your boyfriend's love for you should not be judged by the number of times he tells you he loves you. Most men will show their love in deeds, not words.

Of course, you will get the results you want more quickly by reinforcing good behavior than by punishing bad behav-ior. If you really need to hear him say "I love you" more often, when he does manage to, reinforce it by saying some-thing like, "I love it when you tell me how you feel about me. It makes me feel so good." Even though it doesn't come naturally to him, he will do it because he enjoys pleas-ing you.

He Can Communicate at Work, Why Can't He Talk at Home?

We know that communication is the key to any successful relationship. All successful relationships are based on very good communication, and all relationships that fail do so because of bad communication. Unfortunately, men do not like to talk about relationship issues with their girlfriends even though they realize how important such talk is. It is ironic that a professional man must be a good communicator at work yet may have a difficult time transferring that skill to his relationship with his girlfriend.

Lack of communication causes things that bother you to build up. They may be the most insignificant things, like taking too long to order dinner in a restaurant or leaving the cap off the toothpaste tube. When you allow these things to go on unresolved, they build. All you need now for a fight is a trigger. And once a fight begins, you and your boyfriend are on the defensive and out to win. You will find yourself using all of the ammunition you can and throwing in everything about him that bothers you. Soon you will both find out that there are things that bother you that you never would have imagined. Professional men are competitive and will usually do all they can to defend themselves and win a fight.

In a relationship without good communication, a fight that started over something very trivial can blow up into World War III. For example, Brad was in a relationship without good communication. He was on vacation in Florida when he and his girlfriend began fighting over where to go to dinner that night. Seems trivial, right? Well, the fight escalated and soon he and his girlfriend began pointing out things that the other had done that pissed them off. Neither Brad nor his girlfriend was even aware that these small irritations were building into rage. They never spoke about their problems, so how could they have known? Soon the argument got ugly: Her suitcase wound up in the hotel hallway and she threatened to tear up his plane ticket home and leave right then and there. Eventually they kissed and made up, and resumed their vacation. But it doesn't take a genius to know that the relationship was doomed for failure.

Let's Get Ready to Rumble

Argument is part of every relationship. The trick is in mastering how to discuss issues rather than fight over them and hurt each other. If men are terrible at expressing themselves, women too are capable of deafening silence. For men and women, the silent treatment is the worst. It shows an unwillingness, usually out of pride, to deal with a problem. Men deal with problems every day at work and are not used to having someone on the other side clam up. A man is smart enough to know that something is wrong, but the silent treatment doesn't allow him to know what, exactly, it is. He is not a mind reader. He is used to his male friends, who are straight with him and will confront him with a problem directly. Although men don't like to talk about their relationship problems with their girlfriends, they certainly know that it is a necessary evil and will make the effort to do so as long as women meet them halfway.

Here are some tips about the way men fight that will help you deal with this inevitable part of your relationship. When men argue with each other, they tend to yell loudly. It has to do with that testosterone level again. For some reason, they think if they can sound like Tarzan, they will win the fight. More important, men need to be heard. If you don't listen to your boyfriend, or you talk over him, he will receive it as a slap in the face. Remember, fights are usually differences in opinion. You may not agree with what he has to say, but hear him out. At least you will have a different angle from which to look at the problem. By not listening to him you are telling him that you don't value his opinion and that he can't possibly have anything intelligent to say. This is very insulting to a man and will usually cause an already hostile situation to escalate.

The truth is, men don't like to talk about the problems in the relationship. And it seems to us that women often pick the worst times to talk about such things. During a football game or while we are out having a nice dinner is not the ideal time to discuss problems or hear complaints. More important, men often have a hard time understanding and interpreting what women are trying to say. Men often respond to women as they would respond to their male friends because it is the only way they know. Unfortunately, this method often backfires because women don't want to hear the same things men do. It has nothing to do with how much a man loves a woman, he just does not know how to respond. Sometimes men invalidate women's feelings without intending to do so or without even knowing they are doing it.

If you find yourself arguing with your boyfriend or voicing a complaint and you see that he looks baffled, you might try saying what you need to say in a more direct way. Men are trained in practical problem solving, so we can respond to clear-cut requests. Being direct and yet loving too can pave the way to better communication.

But sometimes women make it impossible for men to respond coherently and honestly. Women tend to ask loaded questions, such as "Do I look fat?" What woman thought up this brilliant question to ask her boyfriend? What man ever responded with a yes to this question? Men are in a no-win situation with questions like this. If they say no, women think they are lying. If they say yes . . . Never mind, no man in his right mind would ever say yes.

Relationships that do have good lines of communication are trusting relationships. If your boyfriend trusts you, and you trust him, then the stars are the limit as to how good and loving your relationship can be. It has probably taken some time for him to be vulnerable, and you have probably been very patient. You have realized how difficult it was for him to open up and have not dissuaded him from doing so once he started. You have probably waited out some frustrating times when you thought he didn't care enough. By allowing him to go at his own pace and not trying to pry more information out of him than he was ready to give, you encouraged him. He was able to see that opening up wasn't so painful, and now he is more likely to do it again.

"What Time Should I Set the Alarm For?": Spending the Night

In relationships that have progressed to more advanced stages, spending the night and living together are topics that inevitably come up. Where do you stay? Your place or his? Sometimes, one place gets favored over another. It may be closer to where you both work, it may be bigger, or one of you may have a roommate and it may not be so private. For example, Rich and his girlfriend spend most of their nights together at his apartment because it is closer to where she works. Problems often arise when neither place is more or less convenient than the other. Then it is inevitable that tensions arise about where to stay, and when. Your boyfriend may feel that he is staying at your apartment more than you are staying at his and demand that you stay at his place more frequently. Think about it—it's common sense in this situation—to compromise and so avoid unnecessary problems.

A man's apartment is his castle. It is very sacred to him. Inviting you to leave clothing or other belongings in his apartment is a very big step for him to take. It is the first real sign that his most coveted asset, his privacy, is being invaded and he might start to think that a pair of sweatpants left on his couch or a pair of underwear in his hamper is the first sign of the end of his freedom. Be careful about leaving things at his apartment. It should be discussed first, because if it isn't, he will feel threatened that you are trying to move in on his domain, and have taken the choice out of his hands.

Brad was dating a girl who was sleeping over once in a while. One day Brad noticed that she had taken it upon herself to leave a toothbrush in his bathroom without telling him. Brad freaked and realized that the relationship might have been getting more serious than what he was ready for. The mere act of leaving a toothbrush in his bathroom without mentioning it was enough to scare him off and slow down the relationship.

A question that often comes up at this stage in a relationship is "Should I give my girlfriend the keys to my apartment?" This is it. This is the last thing a man tries to hold out on for as long as possible. Once a woman has the keys to his apartment, out goes his independence and privacy. The lock can turn at any time and the door open when he least expects it. That is not to say that he is afraid of being caught with another woman. However, someone other than he now has complete access to his sacred privacy. His "self time" can be disturbed without notice. It used to be that he could lie around in his boxers, drink a beer, and fart, if he wanted to, in private. He could read a book, watch a ball game, or do some work. A man's home is his private place where he can do whatever the hell he wants. He doesn't have to impress a woman, kiss his boss's ass, or put up with his friends' problems. He can just relax and be himself. Once a woman has the keys to his place, that mind-set changes forever. More important, he looks at it as a major step toward living together, which is also a very scary proposition for men.

So, if you are spending nights over at your boyfriend's

place, don't leave your personal belongings there without asking him first. A guy sees this as an invasion of his privacy. He sees it as evidence that you're trying to move the relationship forward without his consent. Discussing whether or not to leave your belongings at his place is the polite thing to do and it will help you both keep tabs on how serious the relationship may or may not be becoming.

If You Live with Him, Will He Forget the Ring?

Should you live with a man before you marry him? We think it is a good idea, but only if the two of you are on the brink of marriage. Most men we know would never think of living with women they weren't almost 100 percent sure they were going to ask to marry them. It is true that we do hear tales of men who move in with their girlfriends when the thought of marriage hasn't yet crossed their minds, but we believe these guys are easy to spot. The rule is simple: *Do not move in with a guy with whom you do not have an extremely serious relationship. Never make such a serious decision during the first flush of a romance or because of economic imperatives.*

The more difficult question is whether to move in with the man who is committed to you and whom you love and want to marry. The way he sees it, he is giving up his palace and his freedom to come and go as he pleases. He would only do this for a woman he was seriously considering marrying. When we hear women's trepidation about living with men, we want to ask, "Is there something that you don't want a man to know about you until you are engaged or married? Wouldn't you rather find out things about him now rather than after you are married?"

We think men and women who belong together grow

more attached when they live together. It is inevitable that the relationship will grow stronger and the engagement ring will come sooner rather than later. If a man feels strongly about living with a woman, it is likely that he won't get engaged until he lives with her. A woman saying that she will not move in with her boyfriend may very well cause an impasse in the relationship.

The time to move in together is when you are in a committed relationship and are discussing engagement.

Coping with Jealousy

Jealousy is a natural and healthy feeling when not blown out of proportion. You should not be afraid to feel it if you love somebody. As a matter of fact, you should be wondering if you truly do love your boyfriend if you don't feel a little bit jealous sometimes. If your jealousy is warranted, and he is not aware of what he is doing to make you jealous, tell him. Men need attention and need to know that they are desirable to women. This will very often cause them to flirt with other women. He may flirt with a waitress in a restaurant, with another girl in a bar, or even with someone he works with.

Men just love to look at and flirt with women. As hard as it is to realize, it is nothing against you personally and should not be viewed as such. If it makes you uncomfortable, and you feel that it is hurting your relationship, then there is nothing wrong with bringing it out in the open (remember what we said about communication). But pick your time and your tone carefully. Expect your boyfriend to get defensive. He doesn't want to admit that he has been flirting because he doesn't want to hurt you, but deep down he knows what he is doing. He may just be too naïve to realize that you can see right through it.

If your jealousy is unwarranted, then the situation is more delicate. There is nothing more frustrating for a man than to truly love his girlfriend, have no intention of being with anyone else, yet have her accuse him of being interested in another woman. This will definitely put him on the defensive because he is not doing anything wrong. Also, it is a sign that you are insecure. Instead of frustrating your boyfriend by accusing him unfairly, take a step back. Look at how he treats you, see the look on his face when he sees you for the first time that day, feel how he touches you. These are the things with which you may reassure yourself that he truly loves you and that you are the one for him.

Dealing with a jealous boyfriend can be equally frustrating. A jealous man struggles with the thought that someone else can make his girlfriend happier and treat her better than he can. This is a devastating thought for him. It taps into all of his insecurities and makes him feel unwanted. It is also a difficult emotion for men to deal with. They are faced with a trade-off—confronting their girlfriends and therefore looking vulnerable, weak, and insecure, and at the same time being bothered by it so much that they need to get it off their chests. The best way to assuage a man's jealousy is to stroke his ego a little bit, reassure him of how much you love him, and tell him that there is no one else for you. All he needs to solve his problem is to hear how much you love him and that you couldn't possibly imagine being with anyone else.

The absolute wrong thing to do is to try and inflame his jealousy in the mistaken belief that this will bring him closer to you. Making him jealous won't bring him closer, it will push him away. When men are insecure, they distance themselves. If he believes you are on your way out of the relationship, he may very well try to beat you to the finish line. If he thinks you are trying to hook up with other men behind his back, he'll play that game too.

As the relationship grows stronger, the two of you will need to cope with the topic of ex-boyfriends and ex-girlfriends. We believe it is a smart idea, at some point, to get everything on the table. Usually, men want to know a woman thoroughly before they are ready to commit to her. As much as they hate to actually hear some of the ugly truths about their girlfriends' pasts, they feel that they can only make a decision if they know all the facts. That way they know what they are getting into, and can deal with what they need to deal with in their own way. If anything disturbing ever came out in the future, it could be devastating to the relationship. Not only will he now have to cope with some horrifying fact about your past, something so bad that you couldn't even tell him about it, but he will also have to deal with the fact that you lied to him.

It is also important to tell your boyfriend—and convince him—that all relationships with any ex-boyfriends are definitely over. There is no lingering romance, no lack of closure, and no feelings of "what if": It must be history completely. If he senses any leftover feelings, he will stall the relationship and keep it from progressing any farther. He does not want to put himself in any more of a vulnerable position than he is in already. If you happen to run into your ex, be civil but distant. If you even make a date to see your ex-boyfriend one-on-one or with a small group, even if it is strictly friends only, you will drive your boyfriend crazy. He will be unable to convince himself that there is no chance you will get back together with your ex. If you go out with your ex for drinks or dinner, your boyfriend will know that you may have good intentions but that the guy does not. We've been that other guy, so we know what he is thinking.

Once a guy has sex with a woman, he will always remember that when he sees her. We worry that as soon as we have an argument with her, he'll be in the wings, ready and waiting to make her feel better. Maintaining any sort of relationship with your ex-boyfriend or boyfriends can be another recipe for disaster in your current relationship. Cut all ties to your ex so you can move forward to new possibilities.

S.O.S.—Signals of Trouble in Paradise

In order to avoid getting hurt by staying in a relationship that isn't going anywhere, you should be attuned to a man's physical, verbal, and emotional clues that tell you he thinks the relationship is on its last legs. An apparent change in attitude is the most obvious sign that something may be wrong. This can include a change in your sex life. Sex can lack the intensity that it usually has; foreplay, what little you got him to engage in anyway, may be cut to a bare minimum or become totally nonexistent, and the after-sex cuddling may also be dwindling fast. In other words, it may appear that he is having sex just for the sake of having it. He is ambivalent; passion is ebbing.

He may show less interest in your life. He may stop asking you about a problem you were dealing with at work, or he may avoid talking about your family. If he is thinking about breaking off the relationship, he will stop sleeping over and avoid having you sleep at his place. He will make all kinds of excuses, such as that he has to get up early for work or is too tired to come over. These never seemed to bother him before; why the sudden change?

He may begin planning or talking about going on vacation with his friends instead of with you. You may not be invited to certain of his family get-togethers that you would normally have been invited to in the past. Be alert for excuses he may give you such as "It is going to be a short get-together" or "My cousin, whom I haven't seen in two years, is coming home from the army and I want to spend most of my time with him." He may start using ridiculous excuses to avoid spending time with you. He may stop talking about your future together and avoid talking about the relationship altogether. He may say that he can't go out with you on Tuesday night because he has to go to the gym. He always used to go to the gym, but why is it now causing a problem in the relationship and interfering with his seeing you? Professional men dislike hurting women they cared about deeply. As a result, as patronizing as it sounds, they would rather send these signals and let women down gradually and easily.

Again, we stress how important communication is. If he is upset at you and not talking about it, you can open up the lines of communication. A man is not comfortable talking about his feelings, and he may be waiting for his girlfriend to ask, "What is wrong?" Asking this in a soothing, understanding way can be an effective way to get him to start talking about what is bothering him. If she can make him believe that she is truly willing to help solve the problem, and can assure him that the discussion won't escalate into a fight, the chances are good that he will open up. A man can go on forever without opening up, and a subtle hint from the woman will alert him to the fact that it is okay to talk about what is bothering him. This may make him realize that if he doesn't open up and talk about what is bothering him, things will continue to go downhill fast. Until the problem is solved, he will remain distant and evasive. He is doing this to prepare himself for the possibility that the relationship may be ending and wants to brace himself and minimize the pain that will inevitably follow.

However, when it is too late and the relationship is unsalvageable in his mind, there is virtually nothing that can be done. Most of these clues sound obvious to us; however, we are baffled by women who fail to see the writing on the wall. All of the signals are there for them to jump ship and find somebody else, but we have seen so many women hang on to dead-end relationships. They make up ridiculous excuses to their friends and family, who are smart enough to see what is going on. Perhaps they are trying to hold on to something that was once very good and fail to see that things have changed drastically. Or, perhaps they believe there is something they can say or do to win back the man's love. *Once a man has made up his mind that a relationship is over, there is very little a woman can do to change it or win him back, no matter how heroic or self-sacrificing she is.* It is these women who tend to suffer the most in love relationships.

And yet they needn't. Deep down they know what is going on; the signals are obvious. They accept spending less time with their boyfriends and are reduced to engaging in what is only a shell of a relationship. Inevitably, the ax falls and they are left to wonder what happened. It doesn't take a genius to realize that we all try to suppress things that will cause us pain. But it is difficult to understand why women stay in relationships that will inevitably cause them more pain in the future rather than having faced the music and gotten out sooner.

He Loves Me, He Loves Me Not— Waiting Him Out

One of the toughest decisions a woman has to make is when to wait her man out for the engagement ring and when to move on. Sometimes a woman may feel, based on her boyfriend's actions and words, that he may never be ready to get engaged. Sometimes she may be right and sometimes not. The worst thing she can do is to pressure him and constantly ask him about it. Men aren't stupid. They understand the sense of urgency that a woman has as well as her concern about her biological clock and having children. Men struggle with this decision—getting engaged versus the possibility that if they wait, something better will come along. Men don't have the same sense of urgency that women do. Professional men are involved in their careers and realize that as they advance in their careers, they will make more money and have more power. For some reason, men translate this as more opportunities to meet beautiful and desirable women. Even though they love their girlfriends tremendously, they still think the grass may be greener on the other side. Even if Cindy Crawford were his girlfriend, a man would still be out there thinking there was something better that he was missing out on. Society, and perhaps biology, tells him to be macho and to have many women.

A man's sense of urgency about getting engaged may be connected to whether or not his friends are single. If a man's friends are all single, he doesn't worry that he will be left out in the cold. He still has his buddies to pal around with. However, if they begin to get engaged, he starts worrying about being the last one left, and that thought may get him to think about getting engaged faster. Professional men have usually spent many years in college and graduate school. They have spent a lot of time and money and have worked hard to get where they are. Unfortunately, it is not until their late twenties that they begin to see real financial rewards for their efforts. They want to be able to live a little bit and enjoy the fruits of their labor while they are single.

That doesn't necessarily mean that they need to be with other women, it just means that they want to have some fun with their friends before they tie the knot.

Where he is in his career and what his friends are doing are factors men weigh when deciding whether or not to marry. Asking a woman to marry him is one of the most important decisions in a man's life. A man will delay making this decision until he is absolutely sure that she is the right one. A professional man, in particular, has been trained all his life to be a careful problem solver. He is a thinker and a doer. Before making any important decision, he will systematically gather information, analyze the data, and then come to a decision. He does not want to make the wrong decision. Living a stable life is important to a professional man. He knows that if he gets involved in a bad marriage, his life will become a mess. His years of hard work and dedication will take a downward spiral. He wants to avoid the nightmare of a bad marriage at all cost.

A professional man knows he will learn more about the woman he loves over time, so he takes that time to know her almost as well as he knows himself. When he finally asks her to marry him, the professional man wants to be fully certain that she is the woman for him. Ideally, the longer he is with her, the closer they will become and the easier it will be to work things out. This is the case with Rich and Marla. As of this writing, they have been dating for nearly three years. Rich is still doing his residency and does not know where he will ultimately practice. His mind-set is: I love her, she loves me, and we make each other very happy. As time passes, he continues to learn new and exciting things about her. And they are continually getting closer and closer.

If your boyfriend has not yet asked you to marry him, but you know he loves you, don't believe he is stringing you along. If he has signaled his commitment, but has told you he may not yet be ready to get engaged, the two of you might very well be in the countdown stage of courtship we have been describing. If he is very interested in you, loves you, the sex is good, you spend a lot of your time together, have good relationships with each other's families, and talk about your future together, the chances are that you are on the path to engagement.

Reconsider why you need or want to get engaged now. Is it just to get the ring and what that represents to you? Is it societal pressure? Is it family pressure, or even pressure from your friends? These are all valid concerns for a woman, but they shouldn't cause her to rush something that will come in its own good time. The longer a man dates a woman, the closer they become.

As time goes by, and the relationship grows stronger, it becomes harder and harder for a man to picture his life without his girlfriend. Enjoy this precious time because finally, the day will come when he says to himself, "Yeah, I'm going to do it. She's the one for me." You'll get the ring, and once you do, you will be so busy planning the wedding that it will be like having a second job. And your time together will be much more limited until the wedding. So have faith—men do get married eventually.

Eleven

~~~~~~

THE UGLY TRUTH

The truth about men isn't pretty. We know that when women hear how men talk among themselves they wince ("Men are such animals"), or are incredulous ("My boyfriend/husband would never say that"). There would be no point in writing this book if we were going to candy-coat everything we say. Certain truths about men are ugly, but they are important for every woman to know. With this knowledge, you can work with the reality of how men *are,* not the ideal of how men *should be.* And with this insight, you can better avoid being hurt. We do not advocate or defend men's behavior; we are only telling it like it is.

UGLY TRUTH NUMBER 1
Men Use Women for Sex

It is no secret that men have sex with women they have no feelings for whatsoever. If you think you are being used for sex in a relationship, you probably are. Why do we say this? Because if a man really likes a woman, he will show it.

On the other hand, men hate to go through a drought. A drought is a dry spell, a period of time when a man hasn't had sex in a while. A man wonders when the next time will be that he can touch a woman's naked body. Everyone else is getting action, he thinks, and I'm sitting here twiddling my thumbs. What the hell is wrong with me? And we can't even count the number of times we have been asked by other men how long it has been since we had sex. One friend of ours always greets us with the same question: "Have you been getting laid?" If he is in a dry spell, a man may respond wryly and say something like, "Well, I got a blow job three weeks ago." That's the way it is. There is nothing worse than a drought. We fear running into one. We will avoid one at all costs. So, sometimes we have sex with women we have little affection for. We have sex to satisfy our sexual urges. We have sex because we are lonely and want companionship. We have sex to boost our egos. If we were walking through a hot, dry desert and saw a cactus a hundred yards away, we would run toward it and quench our thirst as best we could. When we are in a sexual drought and see a woman willing to quench our sexual desire, we run toward her too.

A single man who is dating women often has a list—on paper, or, more likely, in his head—of women he can call and then see to have sex with. When he is in a drought, that list is blank. This often happens to a man after a steady or long-term relationship ends. He may have had three or four women he could call into action, but now he's been out of circulation and the list is outdated. At first he may despair, then he may try to recycle old numbers. Finally, lack of sex makes him brave. He is motivated to go out, meet some women, get some numbers, and start a new list. He is in a drought and looking for a river or a stream to quench his thirst. If he doesn't find a river, a cactus will do.

One winter Chris hit such a bad-luck streak, he worried he might never have sex again. Every date he went on was terrible. The blind dates he was set up on were disasters. Chris was miserable. He was in a drought. He tried to recycle some old numbers, but that didn't work. Then he met a woman at graduate school he enjoyed spending time with, and he began dating her. He knew right away that, for the long term, she wasn't right for him. He knew she was a cactus in the desert, but he dated her anyway to enjoy a few months' reprieve from the hot, dry desert.

How to Spot a Man Who Is Using You Just for Sex

As a woman, how would you know when you are the "cactus"? You know when the man makes no commitment whatsoever. You cannot even mention such a thing to a man who is in this mode. A man always knows when a woman wants more out of the relationship than he does, so he will anticipate these conversations and sidestep them faster than a bullfighter avoids an onrushing bull. Such a situation occurred with Brad and a woman he met at a small get-together at his apartment. She seemed to like him, and they got along fairly well. He knew the relationship had no potential, but since he had no other women in his life, he figured he would go out with her. They began having sex, and things were fine as long as she didn't demand anything more than a Sunday night fling. When she made it clear that seeing him only on Sunday nights did not fit with her idea of a relationship, things came to an abrupt end.

Of course, a woman may use a man for sex too. This was the relationship between Chris and a woman he knew. They began dating and had a terrific time together. They were like best buddies. The two of them had an understanding that they would enjoy each other sexually when it worked out for them both. They would go out to parties and bars and nightclubs together, and if neither one met anyone else, they would go home together.

You may ask, if two people get along well, why wouldn't the relationship flourish and become something more? Well, often a man will immediately determine whether a woman has "girlfriend" potential. If the man decides she is not for him, that is the end of that. She may be interesting, but not captivating. She may be pretty, but not his type. She may be good enough for a sexual relationship and a friendship, but not good enough to be his girlfriend. Maybe the woman had sex with this man on the first date, something we caution women against. As a result, his intentions may become less serious. They may not be compatible intellectually: He finds her sexy, but they have little to talk about. Or the two of them may not be compatible at all, so it could never work.

Brad once met a girl out at the Hamptons. She was visiting neighbors for the weekend, and Brad spotted her from his pool deck. She was very tall, blond, and attractive. She was also divorced, at twenty-three, without a job, and with different religious beliefs. She was a nice girl, but Brad did not feel they were compatible. He enjoyed the sexual relationship while it lasted.

How can a woman avoid wasting her time with a guy who is using her just for sex? Recognize him when you see him. A man looking for this type of relationship will only see you if the situation will allow an opportunity for sex. He will not go out with you just to play miniature golf. He needs to have the opportunity to take you home. A man who sees you as only a sexual partner will make ample use of the late-night call. If you don't already know what this is, it means that a man will call you late at night and want to get together. This call typically comes after midnight, and the man has usually had a few drinks. Another favorite for men is the "I'll bring a movie over" routine. It doesn't cost much money, and the man is exactly where he wants to be, near a bed. This is a good weekday-night option and one of Chris's favorites.

You will notice that a man without serious intentions is not very interested in your life. You will find that he forgets many things you tell him and that he doesn't ask those important questions that someone who really cares would ask. In a similar way, he will not make you privy to the things that matter most to him. He figures to himself, Why let this girl inside my feelings when I know it is going to end eventually? He will not call you on a regular basis, and you will find yourself not invited to his family gatherings. He might dangle the carrot of a few intimate conversations or a random invitation to a friend's wedding as his date. But these signs of intimacy are the exception, not the rule. And this man is likely to blow his top if you ever deny him sex.

Just remember, you have the power to tell this man that things aren't working out. Look for the signals and control your own destiny. If you do not mind the arrangement, then by all means, enjoy it. If you are not satisfied, then lose this guy before you become attached or fool yourself into thinking that he really cares.

Do you remember when we said that we would not candy-coat the ugly truth about men so that you could glimpse them in all their naked reality? Well, maybe you should take a breather here because the next section might be a bit hard to take.

Okay, now that you've taken a little rest, here we go.

UGLY TRUTH NUMBER 2
Men Cheat on Women They Love

Why do men cheat, anyway? From a man's point of view, the answer is simple. We like sexual variety. Our natural tendency is to desire new and different sexual partners. A man will always lust after other women despite having a terrifically fulfilling relationship, sexual and otherwise.

Haven't you seen a situation in which a man has a beautiful girlfriend or wife and you later find out that he cheated with a woman who is not as attractive as his wife or girlfriend? Women probably chalk this up to a bad relationship. That is not always the case. A man will have sex with a less attractive woman because he needs variety. Take Hugh Grant, for instance. His girlfriend is a beautiful model. Any man would die for her. But what did he do? He was arrested for allegedly picking up a hooker and receiving oral sex from her in his car. Hugh Grant is not an author of this book, but we can venture to guess what he was thinking at the time. He wanted someone new and "strange." He wanted a woman who was different from his girlfriend.

A man will certainly cheat with a less attractive woman. Despite how pretty a man's girlfriend is, she is still one type of woman, and a man wants variety. A man will stare at, approach, or bed a woman with small breasts if he is involved with a woman with large breasts. A man will do the same with a woman who is tall if he is involved with a woman who is petite. You may not believe variety is the spice of life, but believe us, your boyfriend thinks so.

We have taken note of married men at bachelor parties. They are the wildest, most sexual men there. It is not usually the single men who go wild over the strippers or prostitutes, it is the married men. These are the men who have not had variety or something "strange" in the longest time and are finally let out of their cages. It is really sick to see. The single guys have the opportunity all the time—it is the married men who are locked away and never get a chance to see naked women. The same goes for married men at strip joints. We watch the men who have the wedding bands on. They attack the dancers like no one else. They give them money hand over fist. They act as if they have just been sprung from the local prison.

What is it about variety? What is so good about variety when you have someone at home with whom you have developed a bond, sexually and emotionally? Another woman's body, sexual acts, techniques, and undergarments are all alluring to men who haven't enjoyed a variety of women in a long time. Do you know what we liken it to? Imagine eating the same meal for your entire life. Let's just say that meal was once your favorite. Whether it is sushi, pizza, or steak, if you eat that same meal every single day and night, and someone comes up to you with a liver sandwich, you would find even that appealing. The man's taste has not changed; he just craves something different.

We are not saying that all men cheat. But all men do think about it. Men have these desires eating at them all the time. We try to contain our sexual urges. Our higher-level thinking works to calm down or conquer our instinctive reactions. But sometimes instinct overrides higher-level thinking. Sometimes the temptation is just too overwhelming.

"Grow up! Get civilized!" women say to men. The truth is, we are different from women. Our synapses fire in a different way. For women, we are told, sex is all about attachment, emotional connection. This is true for men too. But often, for men, sex is just sex. Sex is not always about emotion. Sex is not always about intimacy. Sex is not always about love. Sometimes, sex is just sex.

Women often construe a man's sexual infidelity as a symptom of a faulty relationship. This is not necessarily so. But it is important to realize that a man is always on the lookout for excuses, even if just to be able to tell them to himself. Is he angry with you? Now he can satisfy the urge that is always there. Does he suspect that you are cheating on him? Now is the perfect time for him to get back at you. Is he feeling insecure? Now is a good time for him to test his rap and see if he is still desirable to women. Men are good rationalizers. And if the fault lines in the relationship are unstable, then the earthquake will hit.

Sexual Infidelity: The Telltale Signs

We're sure that some of you out there are terrific detectives and can sense when a man is cheating and when he is not. It seems as though women were born with that ability. As you may know, sexual infidelity is not only betrayed by lipstick on his collar or perfume on his clothes, it reveals itself in his changed behavior. Here are some clues to when a man has a secret love life:

His life is out of control and he appears to be disorganized.

Contrary to popular belief, cheating is never an easy thing for a man. He will find himself in highly stressful situations because he is living a double life. This guy will try to keep his extracurricular activities thriving while he is attempting to satisfy his woman on a day-to-day basis. He will always be worried about covering his tracks. He is trying to maintain a juggling act, and the strain will show. You might notice that he seems more harried than usual. And there may be other changes. He may be becoming more secretive.

When a couple is involved in a committed relationship, they are usually open with each other. A man will not be upset by your snooping through his little black book, nor will he care when you are looking at his old college pictures. The relationship is on solid ground and you can laugh together at all your past experiences. If this has been true in your relationship, you may wonder, Why is he now behaving so secretively? Why, for example, isn't he answering his phone in your presence?

Phone operations are becoming more clandestine.

A man with a clean conscience will have no fear of a ringing telephone. A man who is not playing the field behind your back will usually answer his telephone when his girlfriend is at his home. Why should there be a problem? Why let the answering machine get it? We can understand if the two of you are enjoying a romantic dinner, having sex, or are engaged in an important conversation. But when there is nothing to fear from a ringing telephone, we do not think twice about answering it. We will even allow our girlfriend to pick up our phone when it is ringing, knowing full well that there could never be a problem with who's on the other end. We also know how difficult and uncomfortable it is for us to pick up the phone when our girlfriend is there and we know full well that the incoming call could be a problem for us. If a man consistently tells you that he does not want to pick up the phone because he does not want to be interrupted, then we have a beautiful bridge connecting downtown Manhattan and Brooklyn that we would like to sell you.

A man who is cheating worries about playing his answering machine messages in front of his girlfriend. Oh, boy, how many times do we want to hit that answering machine with a sledgehammer when it picks up and we notice the volume is still on high and our girlfriend is in the room. Next we hear a woman's voice and our stomach falls to the ground. What a great home video that would make. Watch the guy do his best two-step to get around the clothing on his floor, hurtling over the coffee table in order to lower the volume on the answering machine or pick up the phone in order to cut off the message before it's heard by his lady friend. The athleticism of some guys is really amazing. Many men will use the old excuse that they like their privacy and that playing their messages would violate this sense of privacy. If you are in a trusting relationship, then this would not be a point of contention. Don't get us wrong, men need their privacy—but playing your messages certainly isn't the same as giving a woman the key to your apartment.

He stops inviting you over but spends more time at your place.

If the relationship is rolling along and you find that the two of you are spending almost all your time at your apartment, and never go to his apartment, then something fishy may be going on. Why do we say this? Because a man will probably be scared not only of the incoming calls but of the possibility of another woman popping by to say hello. It is especially suspicious if it was more convenient to go to his place early in your relationship, and he now prefers to stay at your place. Why the sudden change? Now, if you have only been dating the guy for a short period of time, he may not want to let you come over to his place because he may have a girl-friend. He cannot be caught with you there or allow you to see the pictures of his beautiful girlfriend all over his walls. He will then avoid like the plague going to his home.

Men are very sneaky if we want to be. We know men who have set up voice-mail services for themselves as a telephone number to give out to women when they meet them. These guys will access their voice mail when no one is around. The women they give this number out to have no idea they aren't actually getting the man's home, but are just getting his voice mail. Other men will get a paging service that they can keep secret by not carrying the pager with them when they are with their girlfriends. We also knew a guy who got a second telephone line hooked up to a second answering machine in his apartment. This guy placed the line jack in his closet with the answering machine. The ringer on the phone was off, and the answering machine volume was off. This way his girlfriend never knew he even had a second line to accommodate his second social life.

He cannot make plans in advance or begins to break plans regularly.

Always watch out for the guy who cannot commit in advance to a date or cannot make plans to attend an event with you. We don't care how solid the relationship may seem to you, this guy is probably thinking he needs to keep his schedule flexible in case he needs to make a date with another woman. This man does not know what he is doing from one minute to the next. As we said before, a man play-ing the field when he has a committed relationship is usually traveling at breakneck speed and cannot commit to many things in advance. He will ask you out on dates at the last minute so that he has as much time as he can possibly get to weigh his options for the night.

He takes you out to more discreet places.
When your boyfriend is out on the prowl, you may notice that he doesn't take you out in public anymore. It is not that he doesn't think you are attractive enough, it is because he is afraid to be seen with you. What happens when he is out with you and the woman he took out last Friday night is at the same restaurant with her girlfriends? What a lovely scene that would make, huh? Your boyfriend will take you to out-of-the-way places or decide to order in and watch a video rather than get caught being out with you. A man will avoid sitting in highly visible places in restaurants if he has something to fear.

His condom supply is depleted.
Excuse our candor, but another sign of sexual infidelity is a mysteriously disappearing condom supply. We have a friend who always had sex with his girlfriend while using a condom (as everybody should). She would be the one to purchase the condoms from time to time, and she knew when a new box was bought and when the supply was running low. She began noticing that her boyfriend was in need of more condoms and at a record rate. Unless he was masturbating with condoms on, it was clear that the supply was being depleted faster than they were making love. She confronted him with it, but he said his roommate was borrowing them. She did a little investigating, determined that he was lying, and dumped him.

He has sex with you less often.
You may detect a physiological change in your mate: a lowered sex drive. A man's ability to perform with you will be

reduced when he is servicing others. As we've mentioned, a man would rather defer sex if he doesn't feel up to it. If he is having sex with someone else, he will be less likely to have sex with you. He will probably avoid any situation that would result in having sex with you. His sexual appetite, and his mind, will be elsewhere.

How come your man has become so cool and distant with you? Why, in the past, was he so mad when you went out with your friends on a Saturday night instead of seeing him, and now he actually suggests that you go out with them on the weekends? Didn't he call you three times a day before, but is now so swamped at work that he cannot find the time to call you at all? Remember when the two of you would talk on the phone until both of you would fall asleep, but now he tells you he fell asleep early or didn't hear his phone ring? What are these signs of? This is a man with a carefree attitude. Of course, some men have this attitude to begin with. You should be more concerned about the guys who switch into this mode after having had a more caring or attentive attitude. This man has found someone new to play with. His concerns are elsewhere.

He avoids bringing you and his friends together.

If your man is cheating, he will keep you away from his friends. When we tell you why, you will see how obvious it is. He will keep you away from his friends not because he doesn't want you to get any closer to his heart but because he is afraid that his dumb friends will slip and blow his cover. A guy's friends don't know the stories he told his girlfriend about what he was doing last Thursday night. He may have told his significant other he was working late when in fact he was gallivanting around the happy-hour scene with his new sweetheart. His friend might blow your boyfriend's cover right in front of you. He might describe seeing him from the other side of the bar that night but being unable to negotiate his way through the crowd to say hello to him. This is the boyfriend's worst nightmare. For the cheating man, any inconsistency can cause a riot in the relationship. He is usually so tangled in his web of lies that he himself probably screws up. How in the world can he expect his friends to cover every base if he can't? It is not that his friends have bad intentions, but it is nearly impossible to cover every angle or avoid all conversations that could lead to problems. The lies will eventually catch up with him if his friends are around, so you will see that he begins to avoid them when you are accompanying him.

UGLY TRUTH NUMBER 3

When a Man Says "I'm Not Ready for a Commitment" He Means "I'm Not Ready for a Commitment . . . with You"

How many times have you heard a guy say, "I'm just not ready for a commitment." This line usually comes when a couple has been dating for a while and the woman finally presses the man to commit to not seeing other women, to be monogamous. When he says that he's not "ready," women will then mistakenly believe that this is an issue of timing. He is just not ready to settle down. Right? Wrong!

Listen closely: *A man knows almost immediately whether or not the woman he is dating is a woman he would consider as a girlfriend or potential wife.* If the man does not feel this way in the first couple of dates, he never will. When a man says he is not ready for a commitment, it means that you are not the right woman for him. He never thought you were the right woman for him. And he thinks you never will be the right woman for him. There is very little room for interpretation with regard to this matter.

Think about your ex-boyfriend or a male friend. How many times have you seen him give a woman this line and then a month or a week later meet another woman and fall in love? There is no such thing as "ready" or "not ready" when it comes to falling in love and making a commitment. A man might actually believe that he is not ready for a committed relationship when in reality he is. He just hasn't yet met the right woman who will make him ready.

There are so many men out there who are labeled as playboys, players, scammers, heartbreakers. These men seem to enjoy the singles scene so much that a relationship would not interest them. We are telling you, even these guys will be roped by a woman. Deep down, every man wants a relationship with the right woman. Granted, some men are more fickle than others, but we are still waiting for the right lady to walk into our lives. Brad has been labeled a "player" by every woman who knows him. It is true that he dates a great deal. However, when he meets a woman he is interested in, he settles down. It doesn't mean that the relationship cannot eventually come to an end and Brad will be back to his old ways, but when he thinks he has found a woman with "wife potential" he would never say that he is not ready for a relationship. On the other hand, when he is dating a woman he knows is just "good for now," he will tell her he is not ready for a relationship at the present time.

It's not a good idea to gamble on a man who says he's not ready because he probably never will be—with you. Of course, if a man has signaled his commitment but has cold feet about becoming engaged, that's a different matter. See chapter 10 for advice on whether or not to wait for the ring.

What we are talking about here is a man who will not commit to monogamy because he thinks that you are only a "good for now" girl. As we've said, men know when the relationship really isn't going anywhere. Again, we're not proud to say this, but we have been in relationships that we knew weren't going anywhere but continued them anyway despite the fact that the woman on the other end had hopes or actually believed it was working out.

Let's begin with the man who *always* needs to hang out with his friends. He is probably very close to these friends, and he tells you that you cannot try to come between them. He will explain how you must accept the fact that he must see his friends very often, every weekend, in fact. Now here's the truth: Male bonding is very important, but something else is going on here. He doesn't think of you as his girlfriend. A man who really likes a woman will tell his buddies to get lost so he can spend the time with his girlfriend. Every man wants a woman with whom he can spend a significant amount of time. He has been hanging out with his friends for years; a woman with whom he can hang out and enjoy life would be a nice change. You may think you are the right woman for him but wonder why he needs so much time with his friends; you should see the writing on the wall. Don't let all his phony explanations fool you.

Consider this conversation for a moment.

BRAD: I never go out with women on weekends.

GIRLFRIEND: What guy doesn't go out on dates on the weekends?

BRAD: I just don't.

GIRLFRIEND: I never heard of such a thing. . . . Then what do you do on weekends?

BRAD: I see business clients or I go out with my friends; please don't give me a hard time about this.

GIRLFRIEND: Haven't you ever heard that Saturday night is date night in Manhattan?

BRAD: That is the most absurd thing I have ever heard. Sunday night is date night; that is the best night to see a girlfriend. And anyway, Sunday night is a weekend night too.

That was a real conversation Brad had with an ex-girlfriend, believe it or not. He wanted to keep seeing her but be able to go out on weekend nights without her. Why? He still had a better time going out on weekends with other women or with his buddies. He felt a weekend night was too big a night to give up for her. Was he up to no good on those weekend nights? Probably. He wasn't going to lie to her, but he figured he might just grow out of it. He never did, at least not with her.

The weekend-night thing is usually a big issue for men. Weekend nights are more fun with a terrific woman on your arm. All men believe this. The problem arises when you are not truly interested in a woman and you still want the opportunity to meet other women. The best time to do this is on weekends, of course. But most women think the best time for a date is a weekend night. This is the conflict. How is a man supposed to go out and meet other single women if he's on a date? Once in a while a man in this situation will toss his woman a bone by saying, "Okay, we'll go out next Saturday night." They will go out that night, but the man's stomach will actually be churning, for fear that he is missing a great opportunity for fun with his friends. The Saturday night he "gives up" will feel like the best possible night to meet the woman of his dreams. It will be the night that the best party is scheduled, or his friends will be meeting a group of models, or something like that. Of course, in reality the party will consist of a bunch of guys drinking beer out of a warm foam-filled keg. This man is not thinking rationally, but it is how a man thinks about dating on a weekend when he is not totally into the woman he is with.

There are times when a man will continue to date a woman once or twice a week but never any more. He may even go out with her on weekends, but never more than once or twice a week in total. The theory is the same in this situation. When a man is crazy about you, he will want to see you more often. Men are not much different than women when it comes to this. He will want the relationship to move forward just as you might when you are into a guy. If he consistently sees you only once a week for a long period of time, understand that he is probably still playing the field. His eyes are still open, so to speak, and he really does not see you in the "girlfriend" light. And he probably never will.

UGLY TRUTH NUMBER 4
A Woman's Looks Are Almost Everything

We know you suspect how important a woman's looks are to a man—but you never wanted to actually believe it was true. A woman's looks mean everything to a man. On first meeting a woman, a man judges her by how attractive she is—to him. If a man doesn't find a woman attractive, forget about anything and everything. Of course, attractiveness means different things to different guys. You don't have to be drop-dead gorgeous. He just needs to be physically drawn to you. Men are visual and are driven by what they see. Examples are everywhere. Just watch men walking down a crowded sidewalk staring at women going by. We all know how bad some construction workers are. They will rate women out loud as they pass. Men in suits may be more discreet, but underneath the clothing they are still the same animal—man.

This may sound ugly, but again, it is the truth. If you have a beautiful sister, rest assured that your boyfriend is having thoughts about sex with her. There is no denying this. And don't ask your boyfriend if this is true because he will lie through his teeth. Let us take this one step further. Even if your sister isn't better looking than you are, he is probably still imagining jumping into the sack with her.

If you thought it was a good idea to put up all those pictures of you and your friends at your last birthday party, on a vacation in Europe, or at sorority events, you are wrong. Unless, of course, you don't mind your boyfriend staring at your friends like a mental patient and imagining . . . well, you know.

This brings us to a funny story that a friend once told us. He remembers going out with a woman who had very pretty friends he never actually met. He just saw pictures of them hanging on the wall in the apartment of the woman he was dating. He asked her if he could set one of her friends up with a friend of his for a blind date. She wanted to know what the friend looked like before she got one of her friends involved in this. He told her that this friend of his looked a lot like he did and that everyone always commented on how they looked like brothers. This guy was handsome, and she agreed to tell her friend about him. To make a long story short, she gave him her friend's telephone number and this guy himself called and went on the date with her; he continued to date both of them for a period of weeks. They never knew that they were dating the same guy. This is the ultimate scam, but it proves that men will do anything to meet a pretty girl.

When a man goes to a woman's home to meet her for a blind date, the night is won or lost based on how good-looking he finds her to be. For example, Brad met a woman for a blind date at a restaurant. He had never met her before, and they both decided they would just meet at the restaurant. Brad got there first and indicated to the maître d' that a woman was coming to meet him and that she should be brought to his table. Well, when she arrived, Brad was not very impressed with her looks. He went to the bathroom, and on his way there he got the waiter's attention and gave him his credit card. The waiter asked why he was giving it to him before the meal. Brad indicated that as soon as the main dish was taken away he wanted the bill on the table and the charge already run through. Brad did not want to spend an extra minute on this date.

There is nothing anyone can do about the fact that a woman's looks are everything at the beginning of a relationship. Do the best you can with what you've got. There is a kind of freedom in knowing that a man is either attracted to your looks or he isn't. He either feels the immediate spark or he doesn't. And know that it is also true that when a man loves a woman, she becomes more beautiful to him.

UGLY TRUTH NUMBER 5

If Men Didn't Have to Marry, We Wouldn't

A man feels very nervous about committing to any one woman. He may love you, he may even think he wants to spend the rest of his life with you, but he really hates to sign on the dotted line. If society didn't mandate that a man must marry, he wouldn't.

When a man considers marriage, the first thing he thinks about is not being able to have sex with other women. Every other adjustment is tiddledywinks compared to that restriction. His whole body, his whole mind, his whole self recoils from this idea. He may not have made love to another woman aside from you in years, he may be wildly in love with you, but it doesn't matter. The thought of making that vow of fidelity fills him with fear and trembling.

A man considers marriage only because he knows the woman he loves is considering it, not because he wants to. He knows she expects it; he knows it's the "right" thing to do; he knows if he doesn't propose, he may lose her. As he considers whether or not to pop the question, he does not think of all the gains marrying the woman he loves will bring him. No. He thinks of all the negatives. Men hate to have their freedom restricted. We think to ourselves that a prudent businessman would never enter into such a long-term contract with so many restrictions. We think, every day of our adult lives, that we have been geared toward chasing, touching, and loving many women. How will we be able to stifle that urge? It is as if someone had told us, "Starting tomorrow, you are going to have to walk on your hands for the rest of your life."

Committing to marriage goes against men's natural instincts. Men have to force themselves to marry.

These truths about men are ugly, but they are important for every woman to know. The reality is that a man's sex urge drives him. It is what drives him toward all women he desires. It is what drives him toward you. Men's sexual instinct is an underlying aspect of "guyness" women know about but tend to forget, gloss over, or deny. Women would do better to keep this ugly truth in their line of vision.

Women would do best knowing the reality of men's desires and fears, because once you know what a man wants, he's yours.

To contact the authors of *What Men Want*, please write:

What Men Want
1562 First Avenue
Suite 303
New York, NY 10028

Or visit our website at:

www.whatmenwant.com